11032

92
FORD

Randolph, Sallie G.

Gerald R. Ford,
president

$13.85

5021

DATE			

GERALD R. FORD, PRESIDENT

Other titles in this series:

FIVE FIRST LADIES:
A Look into the Lives of Nancy Reagan,
Rosalynn Carter, Betty Ford, Pat
Nixon, and Lady Bird Johnson
by Elizabeth S. Smith

JIMMY CARTER, PRESIDENT
by Betsy Covington Smith

**LYNDON BAINES JOHNSON,
PRESIDENT**
by John Devaney

Presidential Biography Series

GERALD R. FORD, PRESIDENT

Sallie G. Randolph

Walker and Company
New York

First published in the United States of America
in 1987 by the Walker Publishing Company, Inc.

Published simultaneously in Canada by Beaverbooks,
Limited, Pickering, Ontario.

Library of Congress Cataloging-in-Publication Data

Randolph, Sallie G.
  Gerald R. Ford, president.

  (Presidential biography series)
  Includes index.
  1. Ford, Gerald R., 1913–   —Juvenile literature.
2. Presidents—United States—Biography—Juvenile
literature.   I. Title.   II. Series.
E866.R36   1987   973.927′092′4 [B]   86-16333
ISBN 0-8027-6666-8
ISBN 0-8027-6667-6 (lib. bdg.)

Book Design by Teresa M. Carboni

Printed in the United States of America

10 9 8 7 6 5 4 3 2

Contents

ACKNOWLEDGMENTS

The author is grateful to President Gerald R. Ford for permission to quote from his book, *A TIME TO HEAL: AN AUTOBIOGRAPHY OF GERALD R. FORD.* The assistance of many others was invaluable in the completion of this book. Special thanks to: Dr. Edward Cuddy, Chairperson of the History Department, Daemen College, who reviewed the manuscript for historical accuracy; Sister Martin Joseph Jones, Archives and Special Collections, E.H. Butler Library, State University College of New York at Buffalo, for research assistance and help in obtaining photographs from the collection of the *Buffalo Courier-Express*; Murray Light, Jean Ray, and Sally Schlarth at the *Buffalo News* for their cooperation in obtaining photographs and information; Don W. Wilson, Richard L. Holzhausen, and David Horrocks of the Gerald R. Ford Library and Museum for providing research assistance, documents, and photographs; Peggy McMillian Chestnutt and Mike Roytek of the Boy Scouts of America for providing photographs and information; Paul Facklam for photo retouching; Annette Gernatt, Jamie Hamilton, Marge Lango, and Larry Schiltz of the Town of Concord Public Library; Diana C. Gleasner and all of the other "write people" from the Wednesday night workshop; and especially—Will Randolph, Alice Glazier, Rich Randolph, Bob Weiland, and John Randolph for research assistance, clerical help, advice, and moral support.

For John

1

The President Who was Never Elected

The swearing in of Gerald Rudolph Ford as the thirty-eighth president did not take place as inaugurations usually do, on the steps of the Capitol on a frosty day in January. Instead, he took the oath of office at a quiet ceremony in the East Room of the White House at 12:03 P.M. on a muggy summer afternoon, Friday, August 9, 1974. There was no triumphant inaugural parade. There were no cheering crowds to throng the streets. And there were no gala parties, glittering concerts, special celebrations, nor inaugural balls. The Ford administration did not begin in high hopes and happy spirits, but in a somber mood of national disillusionment.

Ford's presidency began before the 250 guests assembled in the East Room at the White House. In the front row sat his four children and the family housekeeper. Also present were old friends from Congress, the members of the Cabinet, generals and admirals from the military services, watchful secret service agents, White House staffers and congressional assistants, and reporters and photographers from the White House press corps. Television cameras carried the brief ceremony into American homes all across the nation. And watching over everyone were the stern eyes of George and Martha Washington, looking out from the huge oil portraits that dominated the historic room.

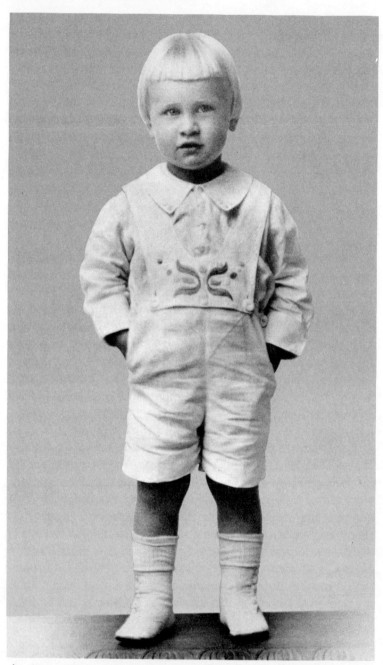

At the age of two, Gerald Ford was a sturdy, blond little boy with an engaging smile.   Courtesy of Gerald R. Ford Library

Warren Burger, Chief Justice of the U.S. Supreme Court, had been flown back by military jet from a European vacation to swear in the new president. "Mr. Vice President," he asked, "are you prepared to take the oath of office as president of the United States?"

"I am, sir," Ford replied.

Ford's wife, Betty, opened a Bible to one of Ford's favorite passages in Proverbs. "Trust in the Lord with all thine heart; and lean not unto thine own understanding. In all thy ways acknowledge Him, and He shall direct thy paths."

Ford placed his hand on the open Bible and repeated the oath in a clear, steady voice. "I, Gerald R. Ford, do solemnly swear that I will faithfully execute the office of president of the United States and will, to the best of my ability, preserve, protect, and defend the Constitution of the United States, so help me God."

On the day before, Vice President Ford had been called to the White House for a meeting with President Richard M. Nixon. Ford walked alone into the graceful Oval Office. His footsteps were silent, absorbed by the thick carpet. The president, who sat alone behind his massive desk, gestured for him to sit down.

Ford was shocked at how haggard Nixon looked, how drained he seemed by the recent scandal. He waited quietly, wondering what the president had decided, still not sure what the outcome of this meeting would be. Nixon looked tired, his face gray with strain, his eyes dull with the pain of a grave political crisis. No one, not even Nixon's closest advisors, knew exactly what he intended to do.

"The president leaned back in his chair with his hands clasped together in his lap," Ford remembers. "His face was solemn. He had been under tremendous strain; he was still very tense, but in control. Speaking slowly and deliberately, he came right to the point. 'I have made the decision to resign,' he said. 'It's in the best interest of the country. I won't go into the details pro and con. I have made my decision.' He paused for a moment, then added, 'Jerry, I know you'll do a good job.' "

"Mr. President," Gerald Ford replied, "you know that I'm saddened by this circumstance. I would have wanted it to be otherwise, but I am ready to do the job and think I'm fully qualified to do it."

"I know you are too," President Nixon said quietly.

The secretary of state is the person in the United States government who is responsible for accepting resignations and certifying them officially. The next day, shortly before noon, Secretary of State Henry Kissinger received this single sentence letter:

"Dear Mr. Secretary: I hereby resign the Office of President of the United States. Sincerely, Richard Nixon."

With the swearing-in of Gerald R. Ford, the country had a new president, one who faced a tough job. The nation had been embroiled for months in a scandal called Watergate. It had started with the arrest of burglars caught in the national headquarters of the Democratic party at the Watergate Hotel in Washington, D.C. The arrested men, who were apparently trying to steal political information to use against Democrats in the upcoming presidential election, were eventually linked to the Committee to Reelect the President, the president's campaign organization.

A congressional investigation turned up evidence that the president had known about the burglary from the beginning and that he had tried to cover up the scandal. Soon it had become almost certain that the House of Representatives would vote to impeach President Nixon. Impeachment would mean that the president would have to stand trial in the United States Senate and, if convicted by the Senate, be forced out of office.

Rather than put himself and the nation through the agony of a trial, Nixon decided to resign. It was the first time that a United States president had resigned from office. And this day had brought another first. After the resignation of Vice President Spiro Agnew nine months earlier, Gerald R. Ford, the minority leader of the House of Representatives, had been appointed to the office of vice president under the terms of the twenty-fifth amendment to the Constitution. He was now the first president who had never been chosen in a nationwide election as either vice president or president.

The people of the United States desperately needed a leader whose integrity they could trust. They needed a leader who could restore faith in government and heal the painful wounds of Watergate. They needed someone whose honesty was above question, who could lead the nation through difficult days ahead. They needed someone who was respected by the angry Congress.

It is said that political success means being in the right place at the right time. That is what happened to Gerald Ford. He was an honest, respected political leader who happened to be there at a time when his brand of leadership was most needed. Jerry Ford had a reputation as a straightforward, responsible, dedicated, and hard-working congressman. He had served his country long and well, and now he was to step into the nation's highest office at a time of crisis, a time when the faith of the people had been shaken to the core. It was, in his own words, "a time to heal."

"I am acutely aware that you have not elected me as your president by your ballots. So I ask you to confirm me as your president with your prayers," he said in his first speech as president. "I have not sought this enormous responsibility, but I will not shirk it. Those who nominated and confirmed me as vice president were my friends and are my friends. They were of both parties, elected by all the people, and acting under the Constitution in their name. It is only fitting then, that I should pledge to them and to you that I will be the president of all the people."

After the somber swearing-in ceremony, the new president plunged immediately into the job. First he met with leaders of the House of Representatives and the Senate and scheduled a joint session of the Congress for the following Monday. He knew he needed to rebuild communications between the White House and the lawmakers.

Next he attended a reception where supporters and officials waited to congratulate him and celebrate the end of the Watergate nightmare. Then he embarked on a tour of the

White House, walking all over and talking to members of the huge staff, always seeking to calm and reassure those whose world had been turned upside down by Nixon's resignation.

Then he met with the press, announced the appointment of a new press secretary, and promised reporters that he would have an "open administration." The whirlwind day continued in the Oval Office, where Ford consulted his economic advisors and announced that inflation, which brought rising prices and weak dollars, was the nation's number one enemy. Reducing inflation, he said, would be a major goal of his administration.

Henry Kissinger, the secretary of state, briefed the new president on the up-to-the-minute state of affairs in other countries around the world. Then Ford and Kissinger spent a grueling three hours talking with and reassuring each of the foreign ambassadors in Washington, sending the message to each ambassador's country that American foreign policy would go on as before. After that, he met with a special team of advisors to organize his White House staff and establish an effective presidency. Finally, after 7:00 P.M. on a long and exhausting day, the president of the United States got into his limousine and was driven through the streets of the capital and across the Potomac River to his home in Alexandria, Virginia. It would be another ten days before he and his family would be ready to move into the family quarters of the White House.

Washington is a city where people often work late on the business of government. Traffic, even at this sunset hour, was heavy; the streets and expressways clogged with commuters. The president's car made its way through the congested streets, moving with the traffic and stopping at lights. At one corner, the presidential limousine pulled up next to a red sports car driven by a Pentagon secretary. The astonished young woman looked up to see the smiling president in the next car give a friendly wave. She waved back. "He is very different from Nixon," she thought. "Maybe things will be better now."

The attractive, split-level house on a shady street in Alexandria was surrounded by a crowd of jubilant neighbors, inquisitive reporters, television camera crews, broadcast technicians, Secret Service agents, and curious tourists. Old friends and long-time neighbors waited inside where Betty Ford, the new first lady, had organized an informal supper and one last neighborhood party.

Early the next morning the crowd outside was startled to see the president of the United States, in light blue pajamas, open the front door and look for the morning paper. Then the president fixed breakfast, as he usually did, for his son and himself. They had juice and English muffins. And, even though it was Saturday, the president went to the White House for another long day. There was work to do. Plenty of it.

Trust in government had been shattered. The new president got busy right away, picking up the pieces and fitting them with his own personal style into a new shape. The pieces were jagged; the edges rough. But Gerald Ford had never let a tough job stop him before. He began as he always had, one step at a time.

That night, after his first full day in office, Ford lay by his wife and let the awesome responsibility enfold him. The Fords prayed together, then talked quietly about the days and years ahead. "We can do it," they told each other.

As an Eagle Scout in his boyhood, Gerald Ford had always taken the scout motto, "Be Prepared," to heart. Now he was ready; ready to face the world's toughest job, ready to help heal a nation rocked by scandal and mired in cynicism.

"When I was growing up," Ford said, "my parents told me about an old tradition of the American West. A pioneer family would struggle for years to pay off the mortgage on their home. Once the final payment was made, they'd place a special stone above the fireplace or in the newel post of the stairs. They'd call it a 'peacestone,' and its presence would signify that the home was theirs at last. In August, 1974, my ambition was to put the peacestone back in the foundation of America."

Young Jerry Ford, age two, squints into the sunlight in this family snapshot.
Courtesy of Gerald R. Ford Library

2

The Chosen Son

When Gerald Ford was born on July 14, 1913, in Omaha, Nebraska, he was named after his father, Leslie Lynch King, a wool trader who had captured the heart of and married a vivacious young woman, Dorothy Gardner.

By the time Leslie King Junior was born, the marriage was beginning to come apart. King was a volatile, jealous man who begrudged even a smile from his pretty wife for anyone else. "Apparently my parents quarreled all the time," Ford said many years afterward. "Later I heard that he hit her frequently."

By 1915, the marriage had ended in divorce. Dorothy Gardner King took her two-year-old son, a pudgy blond toddler, and moved to the home of her parents in Grand Rapids, Michigan, where she worked hard to build a new life for herself and her sturdy little boy.

Grand Rapids was a bustling city, the second largest in the state, when Dorothy and her son moved there. It was located on the banks of the Grand River, near the spot where the river tumbled through the hills of western Michigan in a mile-long series of rapids before rushing on its way to Lake Michigan, thirty miles away.

The city of Grand Rapids was the hub of a prosperous

rural area, rich in forests, streams and fertile farmland. One of the area's early settlers had been a Dutchman, Dr. Albertus Van Raalte, who had come to America to search for a new home for members of his religion. The fine, flat land, laced with waterways and bounded by the vast Lake Michigan, reminded Van Raalte of his homeland. He decided to stay and establish a religious colony named Holland.

Other Dutch settlers arrived in large numbers and soon populated the entire area, making the Dutch, with their cleanliness, hard work and stern religious beliefs, the most important ethnic group in western Michigan. Their influence on the social, cultural and political life in Grand Rapids would remain strong into the twentieth century.

Furniture making was the major industry of Grand Rapids. In the numerous factories located along the banks of the Grand River, proud master craftsmen fashioned the solid chairs and fine tables that were shipped all over the United States. One young man, Gerald R. Ford, Senior, was just getting started on a career as a paint salesman to the thriving furniture factories.

Ford met Dorothy King at an Episcopal church social and was attracted right from the start to the stately brunette with the ready smile. It wasn't long before they fell in love. Dorothy King, whose marriage to Leslie King had been based on an unwise infatuation, liked what she saw in Gerald Ford. Here was a man with a solid, steady approach to life and firm values, a man who would offer security and an abiding, long-lasting love. So Dorothy accepted his proposal of marriage, and the ambitious young paint businessman found himself with a ready-made family. Ford loved Dorothy's little boy as if he were his own and decided to adopt him. The child's name was changed to Gerald R. Ford, Junior, after his new father.

Little Jerry Ford didn't remember life before his stepfather came into it. His fragmentary memories of early childhood are happy ones of a secure home with his mother and stepfather. Even though they lived in changing times, shadowed by the specter of World War I, the Ford family had a com-

This picture was taken at a neighborhood parade in Grand Rapids, Michigan, in 1923, when Jerry Ford, holding the reins of the "pioneer wagon," was ten years old.
Courtesy of Gerald R. Ford Library

fortable life in bustling Grand Rapids.

The automobile was beginning to replace the horse as the major source of transportation, and the state of Michigan was poised on the brink of becoming capital of the automobile industry. One of Ford's early memories was of a neighbor's Franklin "air cooled" auto. It fascinated all the neighborhood children, who would watch enviously as the stately car drove down their street, moving fast as the wind, it seemed, at ten or fifteen miles an hour. Oh, how Jerry and his playmates longed for a ride in an automobile!

The Ford family lived near one of the last fire halls in the city that used horse-drawn equipment, and Jerry loved to run to the station, when the alarms blared, to watch as the huge doors swung apart and the teams of horses charged out, pulling the pumpers behind, fire bells clanging.

For his first five years, Jerry Ford was an only child, but he was never lonely. He was big and strong for his age and more than able to keep up with the older neighborhood children. The paint business was going well, and the family acquired a car of its own, an open touring car that was used for Sunday excursions to the countryside and for an occasional vacation in Florida.

On the day after Jerry's fifth birthday, a baby brother, Thomas, was born. Another brother, Richard, was born when Jerry was ten, and James, the youngest of the four boys, came along when Jerry was fourteen. Mr. and Mrs. Ford raised them all with loving discipline.

"As a child I had a hot temper, which Mother taught me to control—most of the time," Ford remembers. She was a strict disciplinarian who often sent Jerry to his room when he did something wrong. He would have to stay there until he was ready to come downstairs and "discuss rationally" whatever it was he had done.

"I never once doubted her love," he says. "A stout, big-boned woman with an attractive face, she was the most selfless person I have ever known. Because she made other people's problems *her* problems, she had thousands of friends."

Mrs. Ford, like most American women of the 1920s and 1930s, believed that her first duty in life was to her family. She was a wonderful cook, well-known for her specialty, homemade caramel candy. She was proud of Jerry and her other three sons and devoted a great deal of her time to keeping them well-fed, clean, and well-dressed. With four active boys, she fought an unending battle.

Somehow she managed to find time for community service as well. She was a member of the Grace Episcopal Church Guild, the Grand Rapids Garden Club, the Daughters of the American Revolution, and many other civic and charitable groups. She supported the local symphony and helped raise funds for charity, often contributing home-baked bread to bazaars and baked-goods sales.

"When she wasn't attending meetings, she was baking or sewing for needy families," Ford says. "Having the family together for major holidays like Thanksgiving or Christmas would fill her with joy, and she wasn't shy about expressing it. And if a relative or neighbor suffered in any way, she would be reduced to tears."

Jerry Ford's stepfather, a quiet, big-boned man, was perhaps the biggest influence on Jerry's life. "He didn't display his emotions quite so openly, but I know he felt them just as deeply." Ford recalls. He was a leader in his community, active as a church vestryman, a Mason, a Shriner, an Elk, and a strong supporter of the Boy Scouts.

He was one of the first directors of an early program for ghetto youth, a recreation center located in one of Grand Rapids's tough neighborhoods. He helped to establish a summer camp for underprivileged children and was a generous giver of both time and money to help young people whenever he could.

Mr. Ford, to his regret, had never been able to finish high school, so he had strong feelings about the value of a good education. He often reminded his sons about the importance of trying their best in school. He believed that sound knowledge, fair dealing, and hard work were the ways to succeed in business and in life.

"He had the straightest shoulders I have ever seen," Ford says. "As a disciplinarian he was every bit as strict as Mother. A man of impeccable integrity, he drilled into me and my three half brothers the importance of honesty. In fact, he and Mother had three rules: tell the truth, work hard, and come to dinner on time—and woe unto any of us who violated those rules."

Gerald R. Ford, Junior, acquired a childhood nickname, Junie, short for Junior, and started kindergarten at his neighborhood school, which he remembers as an old, three-story building with a gravel playground in the back where, even

The twelve-year-old "Junie" Ford poses, with his golf clubs, outside his Grand Rapids home in 1925.
Courtesy of Gerald R. Ford Library

at that early age, "I remember playing softball and football and coming home with a dirty face, torn clothes, and skinned knees and elbows."

Jerry and his playmates found many ways to pass the time. Their favorite games were popular ones like tag and hide-and-seek. Sometimes they put on makeshift carnivals and shows or paraded up and down the sidewalks of their shady street. They played a lot of ball and climbed a lot of trees and, to the consternation of some neighbors, made a lot of noise.

By the time World War I ended, Gerald Ford, Senior, was prospering as a paint salesman at the Grand Rapids Wood Finishing Company, and he had started a small coal business with his brother-in-law as well. The family bought its first home on Rosewood Avenue in the prosperous neighborhood of East Grand Rapids. Junie Ford transferred to East Grand Rapids Elementary School, where he made new friends easily.

Family life was busy and pleasant for the Fords. Although most of Junie's friends were of Dutch ancestry and members of strict churches where work or play was not allowed on the Sabbath and such activities as drinking, card-playing, dancing and going to the movies were forbidden altogether, Jerry's family attended the Episcopal Church.

Sunday was a family day for the Fords. After church on Sundays was expedition time. Mrs. Ford would often pack a picnic lunch, and the family would climb into the touring car. With Jerry happily ensconced on the front seat by his father, as he always thought of the senior Ford, his mother and brothers in the back, they would head for an adventure.

Sometimes they drove to the Lake Michigan beaches, where the boys played happily among the dunes for hours, scrambling up each mountain of sand and sliding gleefully down. Jerry loved to run along the shore at the water's edge, trying to keep as close to it as possible without letting the waves catch his toes. It was the most fun of all when there had been an overnight storm and the breakers thundered in with the power of an ocean.

Eagle Scout Gerald Ford, age sixteen, with the Scout Honor Guard at Mackinac Island State Park, Michigan, 1929.
Courtesy of Gerald R. Ford Library

One of Junie's favorite destinations was the local zoo. Another was the nearby park with wooded hills and a maze of pathways where the boys would chase around, stalking imaginary game or fighting make-believe wars.

Sometimes they spent the afternoon playing ball. Dad Ford loved the outdoors, so Jerry and his brothers learned to swim, fish, golf, and play ball at an early age. As soon as each one was old enough, the Ford boys were introduced to organized sports.

Jerry loved athletics and was good at most sports. He was encouraged by his stepfather to play hard, play well, play fair, and play with everything he had. "Athletics, my parents kept saying, built a boy's character," Ford remembers.

Hard work was a part of the Ford family life as well. Jerry was expected to do his share of the household chores. He was the one who cut the grass, raked leaves, and shoveled snow. He also took his regular turn at doing the dishes, taking out the trash, and dusting the baseboards.

All the boys had to keep their rooms clean and pitch in with big jobs like cleaning out the garage. As soon as he was old enough, Jerry was expected to keep the coal furnace running. That involved removing the ashes and shoveling in the coal first thing in the morning. The last thing before bed each night, he would carefully bank the fire so it would keep burning until morning.

Being in business always involves an element of risk, as Jerry learned firsthand when Dad Ford suffered some serious financial setbacks in 1921. The bank foreclosed on the Rosewood Avenue house, and the family had to move to a rented house on Union Avenue. Although there wasn't much money, the Ford family life continued to be happy and secure.

"Neither of my parents could be described as 'secure' economically," Ford remembers. "But emotionally both were very secure, and if I retain that characteristic today, I owe it to them."

3

Growing Up in Grand Rapids

During Jerry's early school years, he developed a stuttering problem. "Some words gave me fits, and it would take me forever to get them out," he remembers. "I don't know what caused the problem—eventually, at the age of ten, it went away—but it may have been related to my ambidexterity.

"For as long as I can remember, I have been left-handed when I've been sitting down and right-handed standing up. As strange as this may sound, I'd throw a football with my right hand and write with my left. It seemed perfectly natural to me."

But it didn't seem natural to Jerry's early teachers, who, according to the thinking of the times, tried to get the boy to use his right hand for writing. Experts now think that Ford was correct about the stuttering having something to do with trying to use his right hand for everything.

Even though he wanted to please his teachers, Jerry couldn't make himself remember to use his right hand. It just didn't feel comfortable. He would try, but forget. "After awhile they gave up," he says, "and I continued switching hands as I'd done before."

Even as an adult, Jerry Ford would continue to have small problems with his speech. Some words were hard for him to pronounce, and other public speaking skills didn't come easily. But, typically, his lack of skill didn't stop him from trying. He never became a great orator, but did become a fairly good speech maker. It took determination. And fierce determination was one of his strongest characteristics.

When he was twelve years old, Junie joined Boy Scout Troop 15, which met at Trinity United Methodist Church in Grand Rapids. His dad had been active in Scouting, and Jerry had long looked forward to becoming a Scout. His Scoutmaster, Charles Kindel, recognized Jerry's ability and encouraged him to develop his leadership skills.

"I could tell right off that Jerry would become an important person. He was a born leader," Scoutmaster Kindel would say many years later, when the boy he had started on the path of leadership had become the president of the United States.

Scoutmaster Kindel encouraged all his scouts to work their way up the ladder of the Scouting program to the highest and toughest rank to achieve, that of Eagle Scout.

"One of the proudest moments of my life came in the Court of Honor when I was awarded the Eagle Scout badge," Ford says. "I still have that badge. It is a treasured possession."

Jerry remained a Scout for six years. He earned twenty-seven merit badges, worked as a member of the staff at Camp Shawondossee, and became the first Scout from Grand Rapids to serve in the Honor Guard of Michigan's governor at the summer capital on Mackinac Island.

"My early years as a Boy Scout were invaluable in helping to shape the course of my later life," Ford wrote after he had become president.

"The three great principles which scouting encourages— self-discipline, teamwork, and moral and patriotic values— are the building blocks of character. By working for these principles, those who belong to and support the Boy Scouts of America add greatly to the vitality of our society and to the future well-being of its people."

Sports also continued to be a big part of Jerry's life. His enjoyment of competition, combined with his natural athletic ability and his determination to succeed through teamwork and practice, made him a formidable athlete. He played sand-lot and school baseball and, for a time, like many boys of his age, dreamed of becoming a major league baseball star.

"I used to study those A.J. Leach professional baseball summaries for hours," he told a reporter. "Those statistics fascinated me. I loved baseball."

One thing he learned through athletics was to leave the competition and the rivalry on the playing field. Play as hard a game as you can. Be a tough competitor. But, after the game, put the competition aside.

"By the time I entered seventh grade," he says, "I was becoming aware of the deep emotions rivalries can stir. Some-times the competition stemmed from an effort to win the attention of a girl; or it emanated from a natural desire to outperform others in sports. The fact of the matter was that several of my classmates hated each other. Because of this, I developed a philosophy that has sustained me ever since. Everyone, I decided, had more good qualities than bad. If I understood and tried to accentuate those good qualities in others, I could get along much better. Hating or even disliking people because of their bad qualities, it seemed to me, was a waste of time."

In school, Jerry was an above-average student. He worked hard for his reasonably good grades in chemistry and other science classes, really struggled to get Cs in Latin, which he hated, found math easy, and excelled in history and govern-ment, which he loved.

He attended South High School in Grand Rapids and, by the time he was a sophomore, had begun to make a name for himself as a center on the city championship football team. His coach, the burly Cliff Gettings, was a tough taskmaster who wouldn't accept anything but the very best effort from his players.

"I remember the hours I spent learning to center the ball with speed and accuracy," Ford says. With the wing for-mation football favored by Coach Gettings, "the center was forced to view everything upside down. The opposing line-

Gerald R. Ford, Senior, with sons (clockwise) Thomas, Gerald, Richard, and James, on the front steps of their Grand Rapids home in 1929, when Gerald R. Ford, Junior, was about seventeen years old.
Courtesy of Gerald R. Ford Library

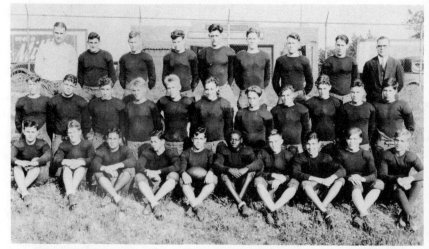

The state champion Grand Rapids South High School football team in 1930. Jerry Ford (middle row, fifth from left) played center and was named to the All-State team two years running. Courtesy of Gerald R. Ford Library

man had the jump on you and to carry out your blocking assignment you had to be very quick. You also had to perfect different types of snaps."

Coach Gettings was a big bear of a man with a reputation to match. His was a no-nonsense approach to coaching. His methods apparently worked because his teams were consistently great, even against the powerhouse competition of the region. Scouts from most of the great midwestern colleges and even from the East used to come by South High for a look at Gettings's players.

But if Gettings was tough, he was also fair, a quality that Jerry Ford could admire. And he even had enough of a sense of humor to tell reporters about the time his most famous athlete, the future president, turned the tables on the coach.

The coach held an early blackboard drill four mornings a week. Any player who was late for this unpopular activity was penalized by being made to run one time around the pool at Garfield Park for each minute late. One morning the coach's alarm didn't go off, and he was ten minutes late himself. He arrived at drill and found Jerry waiting to pronounce sentence. The laughing Jerry chalked off each lap as the coach ran and the team cheered. That was one blackboard drill they didn't mind.

The Ford family finances were usually tight, so Jerry tried to find paying work during the years he was in school. He had a job at the concession stand of a local amusement park; he mowed lawns, shoveled snow, and took other odd jobs. In his last years of high school, during double-lunch periods, he worked at a popular restaurant across the street from school.

It was at the restaurant one spring afternoon in 1930, when he was almost seventeen, that Jerry Ford was dealt the biggest shock of his life.

"My job was to slap hamburgers on the grill, handle the cash register, and wash dishes. One day at noon, I was behind the counter in my regular spot near the register when I noticed a man standing by the candy display case. He'd been there fifteen or twenty minutes without saying a word and he was staring at me. 'I'm Leslie King, your father,' he said. 'Can I take you to lunch?' "

Jerry stood there, frozen with shock, and looked at the strange man. "I was stunned and didn't know what to say."

Jerry's mother had told him three or four years before, when he was twelve or thirteen, that Gerald R. Ford, Senior, was not his real father. Over the years he had heard snatches of conversation about his mother's past and her divorce. But he hadn't really paid much attention.

Today most experts agree that adopted children should be told the truth about their biological parents as soon as they are old enough to understand. When Jerry Ford was a young boy, though, most people thought that adopted children should be protected from knowing about the painful past.

So Jerry's knowledge about his birth was very sketchy. He had accepted the little he knew without thinking too much about it. After all, he had his stepfather's name and, more important, his love. His position in the family was comfortable and secure. His mother's words hadn't made much of an impression. Until now.

Jerry stared hard at Leslie King, his gaze steady and unflinching as he desperately tried to think of something to say. "I'm working," he finally responded.

"Ask your boss if you can get off," the man said.

Jerry's stricken expression must have given some impression of the shock he was feeling, because the boss told him to go ahead without even asking for an explanation.

"My father took me outside to a new Lincoln," Jerry remembers. "A woman was sitting inside; he introduced her as his wife. They had taken the train to Detroit from Wyoming, where they lived, had purchased the car, and now they were driving home through Grand Rapids."

His father asked about sports and wanted to know all about the football team at South High. "We didn't mention the divorce or anything else disagreeable," Ford says.

Jerry kept sneaking covert looks at King to see if he could see a physical resemblance to himself. He couldn't tell. He thought there might be a slight similarity. He wondered if King had shown up after all these years because his son was now a football star. The thought hurt.

After the tense lunch, Mr. King drove Jerry to school in the gleaming new Lincoln and casually handed him twenty-five dollars. "Now, buy yourself something, something you want that you can't afford otherwise." he said. With that, and a quick wave, he and his wife drove away.

"That night was one of the most difficult of my life," Ford says. "I don't recall the words I used to tell my parents what had happened, but I do remember that the conversation was a loving and consoling one."

After the three younger boys had been put to bed, Jerry and his parents sat around the big oak table in the dining room. The three of them talked for hours. "My stepfather loved me as much as he loved his own three sons. I knew how much he wanted to help me and how lacking in financial resources he was."

Finally, exhausted, Jerry went to bed. There, alone with his tumultuous feelings, where there was no one to witness his pain, he let the tears come. That night he cried himself to sleep.

"Nothing could erase the image I gained of my real father that day: a carefree, well-to-do man who didn't really give a damn about the hopes and dreams of his firstborn son."

Jerry was quite shy and didn't have much time in his busy schedule for dates or a social life, but he was well-known in the city for his athletic achievements and well-liked enough to win a contest sponsored by the Majestic Theater. Movie-goers received a ballot each time they bought a ticket to the show and got to write down the name of a friend or deserving young person. The winner got a trip to Washington, D.C.

Jerry picked up enough votes to be the Grand Rapids representative on the trip. He was given a train ticket to Chicago, where he met the winners from other midwestern cities. The group went from there to the capital for five days of touring and sightseeing. Although Jerry visited the Capitol and the White House, he didn't sense anything special. "Back then I had absolutely no interest in politics. The idea of a government career was the farthest thing on my mind," he would tell reporters in later interviews.

During the summer between Jerry's junior and senior years at South High, his parents scraped up enough money to buy a run-down old house, a "handyman's special," in East Grand Rapids. The house was a bargain, and the neighborhood was a nice one, but a lot of work was necessary to make it meet Mrs. Ford's high standards. "The place was in terrible shape," Jerry remembers. "All of us spent nights and weekends trying to refurbish it."

Their hard work meant that, at last, the Ford family had a home of their own. But, unfortunately, the home was in a neighborhood served by a different high school. Jerry was determined not to miss his senior year at South High, where he was captain-elect of the football team. Next year they would be trying for their third straight championship. He got special permission from the Grand Rapids Board of Education to finish at South High, but now he had to find a way to get back and forth between his new home and old school.

Over the summer he had worked at the Ford Paint and Varnish Company, a business started by his stepfather two years before. "I earned forty cents per hour cleaning smelly paint vats, mixing colors, and filling thousands of cans," he remembers. "I had some cash in the bank. So I exhausted my savings and, for the magnificent sum of seventy-five dollars, bought a 1924 Ford coupe with a rumble seat."

That car was Jerry's pride and joy. It got him back and forth to school and to football practice. The team finished the season with a splendid record and won the state championship. Jerry was named all-State center for the second year in a row and received all-City honors for the third straight season. It was a glorious Michigan autumn.

"But then cold weather set in," Ford says. "Because I didn't know too much about cars, I hadn't bothered to pour antifreeze into the radiator."

Jerry drove to school one day, went to varsity basketball practice after school, and came home late in the afternoon. When he pulled into the yard, he noticed clouds of steam rising from the engine. Thinking that it would help to keep the engine warm overnight, he threw an insulating layer of blankets over the hot engine and went in to dinner.

"Just as we finished the family meal," he remembers, "we heard fire engine sirens loud and close. We looked out the window, and my poor car was in flames," The car was a total loss and not insured. Jerry felt terrible about losing his car and about his own ignorance that had caused the fire.

"I wish I could say that experience had taught me all I needed to know about cars," he says ruefully. But later that year Jerry had more misfortune, this time with his father's recently acquired Chandler sedan.

He borrowed the Ford family car to drive himself and some teammates to a track meet. The track team won, but it was a losing night for Jerry Ford. Leaving the parking lot, he backed the big car into a tree.

Oh, no, Jerry thought with that awful sinking feeling that comes right after the crunch. He pulled the car forward and got out to check the damage. *Thank goodness,* he thought,

Jerry Ford (right) in the locker room.
Courtesy of Gerald R. Ford Library

vastly relieved to see that the only consequence of his careless driving was a broken clamp. The clamp that held the spare tire on the back of the car had snapped off.

"We couldn't put the tire inside because six of us from the track team were packed in the car," Jerry says. "No problem, I thought; I would simply tie the tire on the back. Not until I returned home did I realize my mistake. The heat from the exhaust had burned a hole through the tire, and my stepfather let me have it."

Insurance paid for the damage to the car, but Jerry had to pay for the tire. The incident wiped out the last of his savings and, for the rest of the year, he had to get up an hour early every morning so he could catch the city bus to school.

He knew better than to complain, though, and the bus ride gave him extra time to study. He finished at South High with a whole collection of varsity letters and athletic awards. And he didn't do too badly with his grades, either, making the National Honor Society and graduating in the top five percent of his class.

4

College and Law School

Gerald Ford's success in high school football attracted the attention of several college coaches. He was invited to visit such prestigious campuses as Michigan State, Harvard, and the University of Michigan at Ann Arbor. Michigan's famous coach, Harry Kipke, was particularly impressed with young Jerry Ford and launched a campaign to recruit him for the Wolverines.

Jerry visited the University of Michigan one weekend, riding to Ann Arbor on the Greyhound Bus. The coach and some of the members of the football team showed him around the campus and introduced him to other players. Jerry was as impressed with Michigan as Coach Kipke was with him. Academically, it was one of the best universities in the whole country, nicknamed "Harvard of the West." And it had an athletic tradition to match its academic excellence.

But the nation was in the grip of the Great Depression. Times were tough everywhere, and the Ford family had no extra money. How could Jerry possibly afford a college education? The answer to this question was in the simple formula that Jerry would use throughout his life when faced with a tough problem: be ready for whatever might come, work hard, seek help, have faith and take advantage of whatever luck might come your way.

Arthur Krause, the principal of South High, knew of the Ford family's perilous financial position and arranged for a modest scholarship for Jerry, a hundred dollars a year, enough in those days to pay a year's tuition. A generous aunt and uncle, Roy and Ruah LaForge, helped out with a two-dollar check every week. Jerry was able to earn most of the rest of what he needed by getting part-time jobs. Every few months, when he was really broke, he could get a few extra dollars by donating a pint of blood at the university hospital.

So Jerry Ford set off for his freshman year at college with high hopes and big ambitions. He lived at the cheapest rooming house he could find, sharing a cramped ten-by-ten room with a basketball player and splitting the rent, four dollars a week. They each had a desk and a bed, which completely filled the tiny room. Their view was limited to what they could glimpse out one small window.

Jerry did well on the freshman football team and won the Meyer Morton Trophy, a silver football, as the outstanding freshman player in spring practice. He joined a fraternity, Delta Kappa Epsilon, and got a job waiting on tables in the interns' dining room at the university hospital.

Even with this busy schedule, Ford did well in his classes. His toughest subject was freshman English, since he hadn't "bothered to learn" the elements of basic composition in high school. "Every weekend I would labor over the one-thousand word theme due on Monday morning. At the end of the year, I earned a C in the course—and I was glad to get it."

Jerry later decided that, if he had to go back to school again, he would concentrate on two important things, learning to write clearly and to speak well before an audience. "Nothing in life is more important than the ability to communicate effectively," he says today.

In the fall of his sophomore year, he moved into the Deke house with his fraternity brothers and earned his board by washing dishes after meals. Most of his fellow fraternity members came from well-to-do families, and only a few had to work. Even though the fraternity had a reputation as a

Center Jerry Ford was named "Most Valuable Player" during his senior year at the University of Michigan.
Courtesy of Gerald R. Ford Library

party house, Jerry was too busy with sports, jobs, and studies to have much time for dates and a social life. Girls found the blue-eyed athlete intriguing and often tried to attract his attention, but unlike most star athletes, Jerry was shy and avoided any close entanglements with girls.

By the fall of his junior year, he had run out of money, despite all the jobs and blood donations. "My bills for clothes, lodging, books, and supplies totaled six hundred dollars and I didn't have anywhere near that amount," he recalls. Business was still slow at the Ford Paint and Varnish Company, so his stepfather, as much as he wanted to, wasn't able to help out. In desperation, Jerry wrote to his real father in Wyoming. "I never received a reply," he said with bitter disappointment.

Some good friends of his parents came to the rescue with a loan, and Jerry was able to continue his college education. As a football player he spent a lot of time on the bench as backup to Michigan's all-American center, Chuck Bernard. The Wolverine team, famous for its "punt, pass and prayer" style of playing, was an undefeated national champion during Jerry's sophomore and junior years.

"The theory was that if you had a good punter, a good passer and a strong defense, you would always win. If you won the toss of the coin, you always kicked off and gave the other team the ball. You counted on your defense to force them into the mistakes. Inside your own 40-yard line, you always punted on second or third down. If you were near your own goal line, you punted on first down. If your punter did his job, you could pick up 10 or 15 yards on every exchange. Then, if your passer connected, you could score and score again," Ford says of the strategy that worked so well for the Wolverines those two years.

At the end of Jerry's junior year, though, most of the first string players on the championship Wolverine team graduated. Even so, as he went into his senior year as the first string center, Jerry was confident that the team would do well, maybe even by winning the national championship again for the third straight year.

But it wasn't to be. Bill Renner, the team's superb passer, broke his leg before the first game of the season and was out for the rest of the year. John Regeczi, the great Wolverine punter, injured his knee. The strategy that had worked so well in the two previous years faltered without the passing and punting talent to back up the defense.

The team lost to Michigan State, 16–0, and then to the University of Chicago, 27–0. Morale sunk to a new low as the discouraged players slogged through the dismal season that had only one bright spot.

A black track star, Willis Ward, was one of the Wolverine's best receivers. He and Jerry were good friends and roommates during trips to away games. In the third game of the season, Michigan was scheduled to play Georgia Tech, an

Gerald Ford helped pay for law school by working as a ranger in Yellowstone National Park during the summer of 1936. Courtesy of Gerald R. Ford Library

all-white school from the segregated South. The prejudiced Georgia Tech coach threatened to forfeit if Willis, one of the few black college players of his day, participated in the game.

Michigan offered a compromise plan to have Willis Ward and one of Georgia Tech's star players each sit out the game. But Jerry wasn't sure. It just didn't seem right to him that Willis should have to stay on the bench. Should he protest by sitting the game out himself? Or should he play? He agonized for days over his decision. The night before the game he called his stepfather for advice.

Do whatever the coaching staff decides is right, was his father's suggestion, but Jerry was still troubled. Finally Willis Ward himself urged Jerry to play. "Look," he said to his troubled teammate, "the team's having a bad year. We've lost two games already, and we probably won't win any more. You've got to play Saturday. You owe it to the team."

Jerry reluctantly decided that Willis was right and played in the game against Georgia Tech. The team, galvanized by anger, hit hard and connected well. Their 9–2 victory that day was the only one of the season.

A particularly tough defeat to take was a 7-6 loss to Illinois on a miserable rainy day when the field was a sea of mud and the ball so slippery that it was hard to handle. "We must have punted fifteen or twenty times," Ford remembers. "Despite the slippery ball, I had a perfect day." Later the coach told Jerry that the centering job had been one of the finest he had ever seen.

Jerry Ford was named most valuable player of his team that year and was selected as a member of the East team for the annual East/West Shrine game. He also received offers of $2,800 from both the Green Bay Packers and the Detroit Lions to play professional football.

"Looking back, I realize I was lucky to have competed in sports," Ford says. "As a football player, you have critics in the stands and critics in the press. Few of them have ever centered a ball, kicked a punt, or thrown a touchdown pass with 100,000 people looking on, yet they assume they know all the answers. Their comments helped me to develop a thick hide, and in later years, whenever critics assailed me, I just let their jibes roll off my back."

Ford graduated in the top quarter of his class with majors in economics and political science. He was now interested in studying law. He didn't think of himself as the type to become a great orator like William Jennings Bryan or Clarence Darrow. But he was intrigued by something Abraham Lincoln had once said: "It is as a peacemaker that the lawyer has a superior opportunity." That idea appealed to Ford, so he turned down the professional football offers and set his sights on law school.

Once again, the problem was money. And, once again, it was a combination of determination, hard work, and luck that brought Jerry Ford the opportunity he needed. His football coach at Michigan recommended him for a job as an assistant coach at Yale. Ford visited Yale, was interviewed by Coach Ducky Pond, and was offered $2,400 a year to be the assistant line coach if he would also agree to take on the job of freshman boxing coach.

Jerry knew nothing about boxing, but promised Coach Pond that he would learn. As a result he spent the summer after graduation working long hours at the paint factory and taking boxing lessons at the Grand Rapids YMCA.

His brothers like to tell about the time Jerry painted his legs. You couldn't help getting paint all over your hands as you were working, they explained. So you would wear an old pair of pants to work in and wipe your hands off on your pants. Those work pants got so stiff with paint that they could practically stand by themselves.

Anyway, the story goes, Jerry wore shorts to work on one particularly hot and humid August afternoon. When his hands got covered with paint he forgot to grab a rag and, with the force of habit, wiped his hands on his bare thighs. After forgetting the rag several times, Jerry gave up and just let the paint accumulate in a sloppy rainbow all over his skin. It took him more than a week to get all that paint scrubbed off.

With the job at Yale lined up, Jerry applied to the law

school there, one of the best in the country. But he was rejected because the deans didn't think that he could succeed as both full-time coach and full-time student. Ford was disappointed, but he decided to take the job, save as much as he could, and then try again.

The summer before he started his new coaching jobs at Yale, Ford played in the College all-Star game against the Chicago Bears. Usually the college team got clobbered by the pros, but the all-Stars held the Bears to a 5–0 win, an impressive defensive performance. Each of the college players was paid one hundred dollars. Jerry used his all-Star money to pay for his trip East to New Haven, Connecticut.

At Yale he tackled his new job with gusto, helping coach the football team to a winning season record of six and three. For the first time he was able to save some money, even after he repaid the six hundred dollars he owed to the family friends who had helped him out at Michigan.

That summer, with the recommendation of his senator from Michigan, Jerry got a job at Yellowstone National Park. "We directed traffic, supervised the campgrounds, and monitored the feeding of the bears at Canyon Station," he remembers. "At five-thirty every afternoon, we'd load metal containers filled with garbage onto the back of a flatbed truck, then dump them into an open pit a mile or so away. The smaller black bears would come out of the woods first. Then the grizzlies would saunter forth and drive them away. Tourists watched the feedings in a fence-enclosed area from the banks of the pit, and I stood on the flatbed truck, rifle in hand, to make sure that the bears kept away from their audience. Although I saw some bloody fights between the grizzlies, I never had to fire the rifle."

Yale's 1936 football team won the Ivy League title with a record of seven wins and only one loss. Two players made the all-American team, and Ford got a six-hundred-dollar raise. Two future U.S. senators, Robert Taft, Jr., and William Proxmire, were among the players that Jerry Ford coached that season.

Law school was still very much on Ford's mind, so he

decided to attend summer school at the University of Michigan Law School in Ann Arbor and see how he did. "If I received good grades," he reasoned, "I could use them as a wedge to try again at Yale."

Jerry took two tough law courses and got a B in each of them. Even with the good grades from Michigan, the Yale deans were reluctant to let him combine coaching with full time studies. Ninety-eight of the one hundred twenty-five members of the incoming freshman class were members of the elite Phi Beta Kappa honor society in college, they told Jerry. They didn't think he could keep up with that kind of competition, especially with a full-time job.

But Jerry wouldn't give up. He asked again and again. Finally he was allowed to take two courses on a trial basis. When he managed to get a B in each class that spring, the law school agreed to accept him as a full-time student.

Determined to do well, Jerry managed to graduate in the top 25 percent of his class in the company of such brilliant students as Potter Stewart, a future justice of the United States Supreme Court; and Cyrus Vance, who would become a distinguished diplomat and a U.S. secretary of state.

Until law school, Jerry had not had the time or the money for much of a social life, but now, somehow, he managed to fall in love. He was introduced by friends to Phyllis Brown, a student at the nearby Connecticut College for Women. His friends urged him to call her, insisting that she was both beautiful and smart. Jerry, once he met her, decided that his friends had been right.

It was Phyllis who first introduced Jerry to skiing on weekend trips to the mountains of New Hampshire and Vermont. She taught him to play bridge and took him to the theater in New York, another new experience.

Phyllis was a stunning blonde with plenty of ambition and brains to match her beauty. Impatient for success, she quit college and embarked on a career as a fashion model in New York. She even talked Jerry into taking a couple of modeling assignments.

He and Phyllis appeared in a five-page layout on skiing

in Vermont that *Look* magazine ran in March, 1940. The dazzling young couple, both tall, blond, and athletic, appeared in twenty-one different pictures illustrating the "good life." The photo spread showed them cavorting in the snow, schussing down the slopes and, in one romantic shot, kissing each other goodnight in the pale gleam of the dawn. Jerry made one other magazine appearance in the course of his brief modeling career, this time on the cover of *Cosmopolitan* magazine in an early issue of 1942.

Phyllis and Jerry dated steadily for four years. They visited each other's homes in Michigan and Maine and talked about getting married after his graduation from law school. They seemed to everyone like the perfect couple; both were good-looking, smart, athletic, and accomplished. But there were some fundamental differences between them. Jerry wasn't really cut out for the "good life." His roots were deeply established in Michigan, where he wanted to settle down, but Phyllis was determined to stay with her glamorous modeling career in New York. They couldn't agree on their goals and finally, sadly, decided to part. "I wondered if I would ever meet anyone like her again," Jerry wrote later.

5

Law Practice, War, and the Beginning of a Political Career

Gerald Ford graduated from Yale Law School in January of 1941 and returned to Grand Rapids to study for the Michigan bar examination, which he would need to pass in order to be allowed to work as a lawyer in his home state. An old friend and fraternity brother from college, Philip Buchen, had just graduated from the University of Michigan and had come home to Grand Rapids. The two friends decided to start their own law firm.

"Normally, young attorneys sought positions with old, established firms," Ford recalls. But, "Phil and I were impatient and ambitious. We decided to strike out on our own. As soon as we passed the bar, we formed the firm of Ford and Buchen and waited anxiously for clients to appear."

The young law firm started out slowly. The first client, who was billed fifteen dollars for a routine title search, complained about the fee, so Ford and Buchen cut it down to ten dollars. "Phil and I were glad to have any cash in the till," Ford said.

As the year of 1941 progressed, the fledgling law practice

grew. The two lawyers did all types of work, taking on everything they could. They handled real estate transactions and property transfers, estates and pension trusts, divorces and separations, and business and labor cases. Sometimes they earned small fees for defending poor clients whose cases had been assigned by the courts. Once in awhile one of the big law firms in town would refer a small case to the two young lawyers.

Jerry Ford followed a hectic schedule, putting in long weeks at the law firm and spending most of his spare time on community activities. His parents had always been community leaders, and he followed along in the family tradition—working on committees, joining organizations, seeing old friends, and making many new ones.

Jerry also discovered politics. He liked people, and he enjoyed the challenge of competition, so it seemed natural to get involved in the local political scene. Most of the voters in western Michigan were Republicans, so all the action was in Republican party politics, and at the heart of the party was a man named Frank McKay.

McKay was a typical political "boss," a man who didn't hold public office himself, but who controlled candidates, funds, jobs, and other elements of the political system from a position of power behind the scenes. McKay was a multimillionaire whose wealth, his critics charged, had come from years of controlling politicians and, in so doing, landing juicy government contracts for the many businesses he owned.

At one time, it was said, a rubber company owned by McKay had sold all of the tires for the trucks owned by the state of Michigan. Each one of those thousands of tires meant money in McKay's pocket, lots of it. And that rubber company was just one of many McKay businesses that sold supplies to the state and local governments.

Jerry didn't like political bossism, but he wanted to work for the Willkie campaign during the summer, while he was home from law school. He went to see McKay, thinking that the boss would welcome a volunteer to work for the Republican party.

But McKay kept Jerry waiting for more than four hours, then saw him for a mere three minutes. Jerry offered his services, but nothing came from the meeting. Nothing except Jerry's feelings that something was very, very wrong with the kind of politics McKay and his cronies practiced. He emerged from his meeting determined that McKay and his type should be rooted out and replaced with honest leaders.

There were other Republicans in Grand Rapids who believed in the ideas of the Republican party and its leaders, but were opposed to the leadership of McKay and the other "bosses." They formed an organization called the Home Front. The Home Fronters were determined to work within the local party and to clean it up. Ford and his law partner, Phil Buchen, became active members.

But everything changed on December 7, 1941. On that fateful morning, Japanese planes roared over the Hawaiian Islands and rained a deadly storm of bombs on the United States Naval Base at Pearl Harbor.

"I was in the office that Sunday afternoon and didn't hear the news until I flicked on the radio while driving home that night," Jerry remembers. "There was no doubt in my mind that the United States would go to war, that the war would be long, and that everything would change very quickly for me."

In early 1942, Ford entered the Navy with the rank of ensign. He was sent to the United States Naval Academy at Annapolis, Maryland, for basic training and then, like many athletes, to the V-5 preflight school at Chapel Hill, North Carolina, to work as a physical fitness instructor.

The program at Chapel Hill was nicknamed the "Tunney Fish Program" after its organizer, heavyweight boxing champ Gene Tunney. Tunney's athletes were given the job of training a corps of physical training instructors who would be able to go out and whip the thousands of new Navy recruits into fighting condition.

"But there was a war going on," Jerry said. "I wanted desperately to be a part of it, so I wrote letters to everyone I knew, pleading for a billet on a ship."

After more than a year of waiting, he was assigned to sea duty in the spring of 1943. His ship was a light aircraft carrier, the U.S.S. *Monterey,* which had just been commissioned.

Jerry had two jobs on the new ship, athletic director and gunnery division officer. The *Monterey,* with Ensign Ford aboard, headed into the Caribbean for a shakedown cruise, on which the crew learned to handle the carrier and use its anti-aircraft guns. They practiced steering the bulky vessel into the wind for aircraft landings and developed proficiency with all the ship's equipment, from helmets and lifejackets to landing signals and fire hoses.

The *Monterey* chugged through the Panama Canal and into the Pacific, stopped at San Diego, California, to pick up extra planes and then steamed toward Pearl Harbor. She felt, to her crew, like a lucky ship. That would soon prove to be true.

The ship met up with the aircraft carrier U.S.S. *Enterprise,* six destroyers and a light cruiser in November of 1943. Gerald Ford had his first taste of combat when planes from his task force blasted Makin Island in the Gilberts and then attacked the Japanese base at Kavieng on New Ireland.

"We really clobbered Kavieng, waves of planes bombing the port on Christmas morning, 1943, and sinking enemy ships. As a gunnery officer, my job was to stand on the fantail and direct the crew firing the 40-mm anti-aircraft gun," Ford recalls. "The Japanese planes came after us with a vengeance."

During those early days of combat aboard the *Monterey,* Jerry Ford and his shipmates saw plenty of action, with frequent general quarters calls. But Ensign Ford was restless as gunnery officer and wanted an even more challenging assignment.

When the assistant navigator was transferred to another ship, Ford requested, and got, the navigator's job aboard the *Monterey.* Now when general quarters was called, Ford's place was on the bridge, where he was in the center of action.

The *Monterey* continued to see plenty of action, supporting landings on Kwajalein and Eniwetok and thrusts against the island of Truk. Her crew participated in the famous "Turkey Shoot" in the Marianas and joined the task force which was gearing up for the battle of the Philippine Sea.

On an October day in 1944, planes took off from the flight deck of the *Monterey* to hit targets on Taiwan, only forty miles away. The planes returned just as the sun was setting and the carrier's crew rushed to secure the decks and steam away from the dangerous location so close to the Japanese. But, before they could get far, the Japanese planes attacked.

"The noise was deafening as our gunners opened up with everything they had," Ford remembers. "A torpedo from one of the planes nearly hit us and crashed into the side of the cruiser U.S.S. *Canberra* instead. Another torpedo smashed into the cruiser U.S.S. *Houston*. After a fierce few minutes, the attack was over. Both our cruisers were dead in the water."

The task force regrouped and the slow job of towing the stricken cruisers away from enemy waters was begun. But when the sun rose the next morning they were still less than eighty miles off the coast of Taiwan, still within easy range of the ferocious Japanese planes, which attacked all day long.

"Our guns blasted away and finally drove them off. We thought we had seen the worst of it, but our gravest crisis was still to come."

The worst attack came from nature. A fierce Pacific typhoon struck on December 18, 1944, bombarding the task force with furious rain, winds of more than a hundred miles an hour, and mountainous waves.

"That night was pure hell," said Ford, who had deck watch from midnight until four o'clock. "In the pounding seas, the destroyers simply rolled over and capsized, with an enormous loss of life."

After his watch, Ford tried to get a bit of sleep, while wind and rain continued to whip the carrier without mercy. He was up again for general quarters at dawn, then tried to catch a little more sleep.

"I hadn't been back in my bunk many minutes before I heard the clang of general quarters again. Waking, I thought

I could smell smoke. I went up the passageway and out to the catwalk on the starboard side which runs around the flight deck, where I started to climb the ladder. As I stepped on the flight deck, the ship suddenly rolled about twenty-five degrees. I lost my footing, fell to the deck flat on my face, and started sliding toward the port side as if I were on a toboggan slide. Around the deck of every carrier is a steel ridge about two inches high. It's designed to keep the flight crews' tools from slipping overboard. Somehow the ridge was enough to slow me. I rolled and twisted into the catwalk below. I was lucky; I could have easily gone overboard. Then, much more carefully this time, I made my way up to the bridge. That's when I realized the severity of the problems we faced.

"Fifteen or twenty fighters and torpedo bombers were tied down on the hangar deck below. At the height of the storm, one of the planes broke loose from its cables. Every time the ship rolled, it crashed into other planes. Soon, a number of planes were darting around down there like trapped, terrified birds. Gas tanks were punctured, the friction produced sparks, and a fire broke out."

Because the *Monterey* was a converted cruiser, the hangar air vents were inadequate and unable to funnel enough fresh air down to the engine and boiler rooms. Instead, thick, choking smoke poured down the vents, killing one sailor and incapacitating thirty-three others. None of the injured sailors could tend the ship's four boilers, so three of them stopped. The fire on the hangar deck raged on, out of control now. Without the boilers, there was no pressure for the fire hoses, and the *Monterey* seemed doomed, helpless to fight the flames that threatened to consume her. It looked like they would have to abandon ship.

But the skipper, Captain Stuart H. Ingersoll, refused to quit. "Give us more time," he radioed from the bridge of the stricken ship when he received authorization from the commander of the third fleet to abandon ship.

"The ship was still dead in the water," Ford said. "The storm was raging. The fire was uncontrolled. Ingersoll sent a rescue party wearing gas masks to the engine and boiler rooms. They brought out the survivors, kept the one boiler functioning and worked to repair the others. After seven hours of battering monstrous waves, all our boilers were working again."

That was the turning point. The exhausted crew continued to fight the flames with an energy born of hope and desperation. Finally, after more hours of strenuous effort, the deadly fire was put out. The *Monterey* had survived her most dangerous battle.

As the war in the Pacific entered its final phase, Ford's ship took part in every major battle. Ford ended his wartime service with twelve battle stars and outstanding ratings from his superior officers. Their reports described Jerry as "steady, reliable, and resourceful" or an "excellent leader."

When the war ended, Ford went home for a short leave, then reported to the Naval Reserve Training Command in Glenview, Illinois. "Ironically, I came closer to death at home than I ever did during combat at sea," he remembers.

He was assigned to accompany an admiral on an inspection tour of naval bases throughout the South. One of the admiral's top aides was a graduate of Annapolis and an ardent fan of the Navy football team. Navy was scheduled to play North Carolina at Chapel Hill, where there was a base to be inspected.

The admiral and his aide wanted to catch the big football game, so the pilot of their plane attempted to land at Chapel Hill even though it was after dark, raining, and there were no runway lights. The pilot thought he was coming in on one runway, but he was really on a different, shorter one, which had another angle of approach. Jerry's breath caught in his throat as the light plane bounced on the edge of the runway, then lurched out of control.

"Suddenly, the plane pitched forward, plunged down an embankment, and crashed into a clump of trees," Ford relates. The passengers and pilot, badly shaken up, forced open the emergency exit doors and scrambled out as fast as they could. They barely made it. "Seconds after we escaped, the

Gerald R. Ford in his naval dress uniform shortly before his discharge in February of 1946.
Courtesy of Gerald R. Ford Library

plane burst into flames. I got out with only the shirt on my back," Ford says.

Jerry Ford was discharged from the Navy in February of 1946, with the rank of lieutenant commander and a brilliant record. He had served his country with distinction and had seen much of the world, but he was now approaching his mid-thirties. It was time to settle down and build a career.

Jerry and the thousands of other soldiers, sailors, and marines who had fought World War II returned home to a changed America. And Jerry was changed himself by the experiences of war and by the growing up he had done. He had seen and heard and learned.

Many leaders of the Home Front organization had gone off to war or to war-related jobs in the factories of Michigan or in government offices in Washington. Because Ford's law partner, Phil Buchen, had been left handicapped by a childhood case of polio, he was not eligible for military service. He had stayed behind and joined a prominent local law firm.

Dad Ford had been a Civil Defense leader during the war and had, at the urging of his son, become a Republican county chairman to hold the position open while so many of the young Home Front members were off fighting.

Phil Buchen and Jerry talked about reestablishing their own law firm, but eventually decided against it. Instead, Jerry was offered a job at the same place Phil worked, Butterfield, Keeney & Amberg, one of the biggest law firms in Grand Rapids. He decided to take the job.

For a while Jerry was content to coast and relax after the grind of college, law school, and the war. "I was thirty-three, single, working, having a great time, playing a lot of golf," he told Jerald F. terHorst, a reporter for the Grand Rapids *Press*.

But soon his interest in politics was revived. His dislike of the political machine that ran the Republican party in Grand Rapids and his concern that the remaining isolationists in Washington would undermine America's position lured him back into Republican party politics.

"Before the war I'd been an isolationist. Indeed, while at

Yale, I had expressed the view that the U.S. ought to avoid 'entangling alliances' abroad. But now I had become an ardent internationalist. My wartime experiences had given me an entirely new perspective," Ford says.

Before the war there had been a bitter political struggle between the isolationists and internationalists. The isolationists thought that America's security was best preserved by staying out of foreign wars and alliances altogether. The internationalists believed that the nation's security depended on stopping the relentless drive of Hitler and the Nazis. The debate was brought to an abrupt end by Pearl Harbor.

Now Jerry, like most of the prewar isolationists, had changed his mind. "The U.S., I was convinced, could no longer stick its head in the sand like an ostrich. Our military unpreparedness before World War II had only encouraged the Germans and Japanese. In the future, I felt, the U.S. had to be strong. And because a strong America would need strong allies to resist the growing Communist threat, we simply had to provide the money, muscle, and manpower to help the nations of Western Europe rebuild their shattered economies."

He found himself spending more and more time with his Home Front friends. He was also, in his own words, "a compulsive joiner." He became an active member of the American Legion and the Veterans of Foreign Wars, and he spearheaded a campaign to change the local zoning laws so returning veterans could build affordable houses.

He joined the local chapter of the Red Cross and worked on the Kent County cancer drive. He raised money for the United Fund and served on the board of directors of the Family Services Association. He helped plan weekend outings for Boy Scouts and joined the local chapter of the National Association for the Advancement of Colored People (NAACP) because he believed that black people were being treated unfairly in America.

During the war the Home Front in Grand Rapids had continued to work against the political machine of Boss McKay. By 1946 McKay was washed up as a major political force, but some of the people he had helped get elected to office or appointed to political jobs were still entrenched in positions of power.

One of those McKay legacies was the congressman from Michigan's Fifth District, Bartel J. (Barney) Jonkman. Jonkman was still clinging to his outdated isolationist views and spent most of his congressional efforts fighting against programs that would help rebuild Europe. He was a bitter foe of President Harry Truman's so-called Marshall Plan, which would provide money and materials to the devastated nations of western Europe.

Jonkman was "doing everything he could to torpedo constructive foreign aid legislation," Ford said. "Someone," he told his Home Front colleagues, "should oppose him for renomination." The Home Fronters agreed, but none of them seemed interested in the race.

Jonkman, the politicians thought, was unbeatable. His solid Dutch ancestry went back for many generations, and this was a district where the Dutch were the most powerful ethnic group. He was extremely conservative and so were his constituents. And, because he had been in Congress for so long, he was powerful there and in a position to do many favors for supporters in his district.

"Forget it," Jerry was told over and over again. "Jonkman can't be beat. He's too strong and too powerful. There's nothing to be done about him."

But Jerry Ford knew that there is always hope, even when the odds seem to be badly against you. "Nothing is impossible," he told the Home Fronters.

"Well, if you really believe that, why don't you run against Jonkman yourself?" they asked.

"My parents thought I should try," Ford says. "So did Phil Buchen." His friends offered encouragement, and the Home Front promised to support his candidacy. So Jerry Ford decided to tackle the impossible. He decided to run for Congress against the man who couldn't be beat.

6

The Young Congressman From Michigan

Jerry's decision to take on Barney Jonkman for the fifth district congressional seat had the enthusiastic support of his friends in the Home Front, which served as the nucleus of a campaign organization. Jack Stiles, Jerry's campaign manager, warned that if there was any hope of succeeding, that hope lay in surprise.

"Don't tell anyone yet," Jack advised. "Once Jonkman realizes that someone is after him, he'll attack. And he's the one with the power. Let him think he's safe. Let him stay complacent."

"Can't I even tell Betty?" Ford asked.

Betty was a young woman named Elizabeth Ann Bloomer Warren, whom Jerry had been dating for six months. She was a real beauty, with smiling, wide-set eyes and the elegant carriage of a dancer, which wasn't surprising, since she had studied ballet and modern dance for years and had once planned a professional career in dance. Betty and Jerry had both grown up in Grand Rapids. They hadn't known each other before, although they had known of each other, and, over the years, their paths had sometimes crossed. Betty, five years younger, was still in high school during Jerry's years as a Michigan football star. But she often went on dates to the Michigan games and the Saturday night dances afterward.

And when Jerry was home summers from Yale and Betty was back from New York and her dance studies under the famous Martha Graham, they moved on the fringes of the same circles, often attending the same parties and dances.

Both were well-known and well-liked. Everyone in Grand Rapids remembered Jerry for his football prowess and other athletic achievements. And because Betty had been a New York dancer, she had acquired a glamorous reputation of her own.

But then their paths took different directions. Betty got married, and Jerry went to war. Betty's marriage to a salesman named Bill Warren lasted for six years of trying unsuccessfully to adjust to the differences in their basic life-styles. It eventually ended in an amicable divorce. There were no children. Betty received a settlement of one dollar, the furniture from their apartment, and the freedom to pursue her career as a fashion coordinator at the largest department store in Grand Rapids. She loved her work and hated the thought of plunging into marriage again.

Jerry was too busy with his law practice, his community activities, and his budding political career to think about marriage. He and Betty went out often. They really enjoyed each other's company. They liked to do the same kinds of things. They enjoyed talking with each other. That, they told themselves, was as far as the relationship went. Neither of them was interested in anything permanent.

But when Jerry went away for a two-week ski vacation at Sun Valley, Idaho, after Christmas and Betty went on a business trip to New York, the two found that they missed each other terribly.

"I wrote to her every day. I bought her a hand-tooled leather belt with a silver buckle from Sun Valley," Ford says.

Jerry's friends teased him about the gift. "You mean Jerry

Ford actually gave a present to a *girl*," they laughed. "This must be serious."

It was. Jerry proposed to Betty in February. "I'd like to marry you," he said, "but we can't get married until next fall, and I can't tell you why."

Betty accepted the strange proposal and agreed that a fall wedding would be fine. And Jerry continued with his secret plans to challenge Barney Jonkman in the Republican primary election.

A primary election is one where members of a political party vote on who the party will nominate to run in the general election. Jerry and his campaign crew knew that the only way to oust Barney Jonkman would be to beat him in the Republican primary. Because there were so few Democrats in the Fifth District, the election was sure to be won by whoever ran as the Republican candidate. Winning the primary was the goal of the newly formed "Ford for Congress" committee.

Ford announced his candidacy in June of 1948, just before the final deadline for candidates to have their names placed on the primary ballot. Jonkman was so sure of himself that he barely noticed. To the smug and arrogant congressman, Jerry Ford was no more than a slight nuisance, a minor irritation, a young upstart without a chance. Jonkman wasn't worried.

Ford took advantage of the incumbent's complacency and got right to work trying to convince Republicans to vote for him in the upcoming primary. His law partners supported him and gave him time off to campaign. And campaign he did.

From early in the morning until late at night, Jerry Ford spent every second he could meeting voters and asking for their support.

Jerald terHorst, who would one day become President Ford's press secretary, was a reporter for the Grand Rapids *Press* during that primary campaign of 1948. He remembers a rainy morning in late June when the phone on his desk rang. It was only five o'clock in the morning, but the voice

Gerald Ford campaigned for Congress in 1948 by getting out and visiting farmers in the district.
Courtesy of Gerald R. Ford Library

on the other end of the line sounded brisk and cheerful. It was congressional candidate Ford.

"Ready to go?" Ford asked.

"But it's pouring. You're going out anyway?"

"They milk cows *every* day," Ford responded impatiently. "Besides, I promised."

Ford picked up the reporter a few minutes later, and the two men drove through the dawn to the first of seven farms they would visit that morning.

"Four votes in this family," Ford whispered to terHorst as they slogged through the barnyard mud and into the heavy warmth of the huge dairy barn. The farmer, a stocky man dressed in knee-high boots, walked down the large aisle in the center of the barn. On either side, a row of placid Jersey cows watched as Jerry stepped forward and introduced himself. His little speech, which he was to repeat many times during the course of the campaign, went something like this:

"Hi, I'm Jerry Ford, I'm running for Congress in the September primary, the Republican primary. I came by today because I don't know much about farming, and I'm sure you and other farmers have problems that the folks in Washington don't understand. If I were to become your congressman, instead of Mr. Jonkman, I wonder if there's anything you would like me to be doing for you."

Ford usually got a positive response. Often the farmer would talk for ten or twenty minutes about the difficulties he faced. Jerry listened carefully. Sometimes he jotted down a few notes. Then he would shake hands with the farmer and hand him a campaign card. "Remember the name—Ford," he would say. "If I get to Congress, I'll remember what you've told me."

Ford campaigned heavily among the farmers, meeting them in barns, in the fields, in their homes. Sometimes he even helped to pitch hay while he talked. He knew that each farmer he visited would tell others. If he could meet enough voters and make a favorable impression, the word would spread that this young candidate, name of Ford, just might be a good man to send to Washington.

Ford also knew that factories were fertile places to pick up votes and he soon enlisted the support of organized labor. One of his early labor supporters was Leonard Woodcock, who would one day be a president himself, president of the United Auto Workers, one of the most powerful unions in the country.

Ford sought votes among the many returning veterans. Day after day he roamed back and forth across the fifth congressional district, meeting as many voters as he could, asking for support and promising to take the concerns of the voters to Washington.

Jerry considered Jonkman's isolationism to be the most important issue of the campaign and spoke out as often as

Gerald Ford and several of his campaign aides keep track of the primary vote tally on September 14, 1948. Ford's trouncing of opponent Barney Jonkman was the first of many political victories for Jerry Ford. Courtesy of Gerald R. Ford Library

he could about the need to support the Marshall Plan and get the war-torn countries of western Europe going again.

The other campaign workers were busy, too—raising money, organizing meetings and rallies, planning special events, setting up headquarters. And President Truman even helped, although not on purpose, by calling Congress into special session in Washington. While Barney Jonkman was back in the Capitol, Jerry Ford was all over the district, whittling away at Jonkman's once-great lead.

At first, Jonkman hardly noticed the little band of insurgent Republicans who were trying to unseat him. But when he returned to Michigan in August, after the special session of Congress, he discovered to his horror that Ford's name was

*Gerald and Betty Ford on their wedding day, October 15, 1948.
Courtesy of Gerald R. Ford Library*

now well-known. Even worse, the voters seemed to like this forthright young man. They seemed to like him very much indeed.

Jonkman panicked and began to pick fights with the newspapers who were writing favorable things about Ford. The tone of his campaign turned nasty and had the effect of boosting Ford's popularity even more. On primary day, September 14, 1948, Ford achieved the impossible. He beat Jonkman for the Republican nomination. Not only that, he walloped him, 23,632 to 14,341.

Now Ford was the official candidate of the Republican party and faced certain election in the overwhelmingly Republican district. He continued to campaign, of course, but now he had time for other things. Like getting married.

Jerry Ford and Betty Bloomer were married at Grace Episcopal Church in Grand Rapids on October 15, 1948. They had decided to wait until after the primary election. Some of Jerry's supporters were afraid that Betty would be judged harshly by the stern religious fundamentalists who were so prominent in the fifth district and who were doggedly opposed to both divorce and dancing.

One of Jerry's aides told them: "Can you imagine what Jonkman's people would do if they found out about the wedding? They'd probably have phoney leaflets printed up that say 'Vote for Ford' and they'd find a way to work in that Betty was a divorced ex-dancer. Then they'd go around to all the strict churches on the Sunday before the primary and pass out the leaflets to the people as they were coming out of church."

The wedding had been postponed until after the primary, but now the big day had finally arrived. Jerry, to his mother's annoyance, campaigned right up until the last possible moment. Then he rushed in, changed quickly into his best suit and hurried to the church.

His mother was horrified to see that he had forgotten to change into his good black shoes and was still wearing scuffed brown campaign shoes. Worse, they were coated with dust.

"My mother was furious," Ford recalls. "Betty pretended

not to notice, and friends still kid me about it until this day."

Betty had been warned by Jerry's sister-in-law, Janet Ford, that marriage to a politician would be challenging. She wouldn't ever have to worry about other women, Janet joked, because Jerry was in love with politics.

Their honeymoon was a taste of the life to come—a quick trip to a football game at the University of Michigan the next afternoon, an evening appearance at a rally in Owasso for the Republican presidential candidate, Thomas E. Dewey, and a brief overnight stop in Detroit. Then it was home to Grand Rapids and the final push to election day.

Jerry Ford was elected to Congress on November 2, 1948, with a whopping 62 percent of the vote. Even though the campaign had left him in debt and there wasn't much prospect of financial security on a Congressman's salary, Jerry was elated. "I had won a race that no one six months before had given me a chance to win."

He and Betty went to Washington and found a cozy furnished apartment not far from the Capitol. Betty got busy establishing their home while Jerry headed for Congress.

Early on New Year's morning in 1949, Jerry Ford and his newly hired congressional assistant, John P. Malinowski, put on grubby workclothes and went to the Capitol. They knew it was going to take a lot of work to get settled into the office assigned to Jerry, the same office so recently vacated by the defeated Barney Jonkman. A suspicious Capitol policeman stopped them as they walked through the echoing halls of the deserted building.

"This is the new congressman from Grand Rapids," Malinowski assured the skeptical officer. "I'm his assistant."

The two had tackled a monumental cleaning job. They sorted through huge piles of papers and books, the debris of Jonkman's years in Congress. They threw out stacks of old phone books, boxes of yellowed newspaper clippings, piles of outdated reports, file folders full of useless letters and long-forgotten memos.

They lugged countless cartons of trash to the incinerator. They rearranged furniture, hung a few framed mementos on

The newly elected young congressman poses with his proud parents,
Dorothy Gardner Ford and Gerald R. Ford, Senior.
Courtesy of Gerald R. Ford Library

the walls, and set up the new congressman's meager files. It
took hours of backbreaking work to make the office tidy
enough for the two secretaries from Grand Rapids, who would
soon start their new jobs.

Jerry's office was next door to another Navy veteran's, a
young Democratic representative from Massachusetts named
John F. Kennedy. Upstairs was the office of a second-term
congressman, also a Navy man, from California by the name
of Richard Nixon.

Gerald R. Ford's congressional career officially began on
Monday, January 3, 1949, when Congress convened. All new
members of the House of Representatives are sworn in on
the first day of the session. Terms of office in the House last

only two years, with all 435 members elected at the same time.

Each two-year Congress is given a number. Jerry was a freshman member of the eighty-first Congress, the eighty-first since Congress first met in 1789 and saw George Washington become president. As a Republican, Jerry was a member of the minority party, which held fewer seats than did the Democrats, the majority party.

The House of Representatives meets in a huge room, the House Chamber in the national Capitol building on the crest of Capitol Hill in Washington. The imposing room is filled with semicircular rows of seats on either side of a center aisle. Congressmen do not have assigned seats but, by tradition, sit on the same side of the aisle as the other members of their party—the right for Republicans and left for Democrats.

Above the curving rows of seats on the "floor" of the House a circular gallery has seats for visitors. At the front of the chamber stands the Speaker's platform. The Speaker, the most powerful man in Congress, is the leader of the majority party. He runs Congress.

Congressman Ford, idealistic, eager to learn, and committed to a political philosophy that he has often described as "liberal in foreign policy, moderate on domestic programs, and conservative on money issues," took a seat near the back on the Republican side of the aisle and spent his first few weeks watching how things work. He soon learned that the real work of Congress is done by committees.

There is so much business facing Congress—thousands of bills, or proposed laws, to write and consider; hundreds of subjects to study, everything from the workings of the military to the District of Columbia sewer system; dozens of issues to understand—that if every member had to be well-informed about every bill, there wouldn't be enough time to pass laws.

So both houses of Congress, the Senate and the House of Representatives, use a system of committees to study proposed bills, make changes in them, and make recommendations when it is time to consider the bill on the House or Senate floor.

The House has numerous permanent committees called standing committees. Each has a specialty such as agriculture, foreign relations, or the federal budget. Each committee is likely to have several subcommittees which focus on particular aspects of the committee's specialty.

Some committees are very important. In the House of Representatives the two most powerful are the Appropriations Committee, which decides how much money to spend on programs planned by Congress; and the Rules Committee, which controls when and under what conditions each bill will be discussed by the entire House.

New representatives are assigned to committees by the leaders of their respective parties. Committee chairmen are always members of the majority party. The number of Democrats and Republicans on each committee is in proportion to each party's relative strength in the House.

Ford watched, fascinated by the workings of Congress, intrigued by the way the nation's business was conducted. He observed the way the Speaker, Democrat Sam Rayburn of Texas, ruled every aspect of the House of Representatives, a thundering gavel the symbol of his power.

He began to see that the Speaker's job was one of the most important jobs in the whole country, only slightly less powerful than the job of president. An ambitious man could accomplish a great deal as Speaker of the House, Ford thought. As he watched and learned, Jerry Ford thought that he would like to be Speaker of the House one day.

House Minority Leader Gerald R. Ford in 1965.
Buffalo Courier-Express *Courtesy E.H. Butler Library, State col-*
lege at Buffalo and Historical Society, Buffalo and Erie County

7

Growing Family, Growing Career

Gerald R. Ford's career in the House of Representatives would eventually span almost twenty-five years. He came to Washington while President Truman was in the White House, and he served under five different presidents: Harry Truman, Dwight D. Eisenhower, John F. Kennedy, Lyndon B. Johnson, and Richard M. Nixon.

Ford quickly developed a reputation as a stalwart supporter of Republican programs, but a willing cooperator with the Democrats when working together was required to pass important legislation. It didn't take him long to grasp the nuances of leadership in the House and to set his sights on the top job.

While many congressmen use their seats in the House of Representatives as stepping-stones to other political offices, Jerry Ford was content to stay where he was and work his way up the ladder of leadership in the House itself. His success would be due to several reasons.

First, Jerry Ford proved to be pragmatic, or practical, in his political philosophy. He was willing to listen to other points of view and to compromise with adversaries when necessary.

Ford was also a hard worker. He spent long days serving

the needs of his constituents back home in Grand Rapids, studying bills, staying well-informed on the countless issues that demanded congressional attention, and spending a large portion of his time on the House floor. In fact, he had one of the best attendance records in Congress.

Ford was popular. People liked him, both because of his open personality and his willingness to help almost anyone if he could. He was reelected twelve times by the people in his district, each time with a wide margin of victory.

Jerry Ford liked people, and they could tell. He had learned on the football field that conflict did not have to mean enmity. He knew that you could disagree with a friend, that you could agree with an enemy, and that you could work with almost anyone if you were willing to try.

During his first two-year term of office, Jerry concentrated on learning the ropes. He set up one of the most effective congressional offices in Washington, later known as his "people pleasing machine." Folks from home who came to visit Washington were warmly welcomed by Ford and his staff.

An instant camera was permanently mounted in a corner of the office. If Ford was there at the time, the guests from home would be given pictures of themselves with the congressman. If he was out of town or busy on the House floor, visitors were invited to sit at the representative's imposing desk for their souvenir photo.

Every letter that arrived at the busy office was promptly answered, every request honored as far as possible, every concern addressed. Ford's staff scanned the newspapers from home and sent messages of congratulation or condolence to the newly married, recently promoted, or bereaved.

The office staff cooperated with those from home who wanted to land a government job, solve a problem with a government agency, or cut through federal red tape. It didn't matter if you had voted for Ford or not. It didn't matter if you were a Republican or a Democrat, old or young, rich or poor. If he thought you deserved it, Congressman Ford was willing to help you out. And every two years the grateful constituents in the Fifth District returned Jerry Ford to

Washington with bigger and bigger electoral victories.

Representative Ford's stature was increasing with his colleagues as well. During his second term in office he won a fortunate appointment to the Appropriations Committee, where he impressed the chairman with his willingness to work and with his grasp of complex issues. His work on a subcommittee that researched military spending and the painstaking reports he prepared soon earned him a reputation as an expert on defense budgets.

Other Congressmen and Senators found him congenial, competent and easy to work with. Even the Democrats liked him. Although Ford was known as a loyal party man, dedicated to mounting an effective opposition to Democratic bills that he believed to be imprudent and to pushing for Republican programs, he was also regarded as fair and willing to compromise.

During his second term, Ford joined a group of eighteen House members who sent a letter to General Dwight Eisenhower, the immensely popular military leader of World War II, urging him to try for the 1952 Republican presidential nomination. "The leading candidate at the time was Senator Robert Taft of Ohio," Ford recalls, "but his foreign policy views were too isolationist for my taste. Furthermore, I was convinced Ike could win in November and after nearly twenty years of Democratic presidents the country needed a change."

Eisenhower did win in November and would later say that the letter from the eighteen congressmen had been an important reason why he decided to run. Jerry Ford's early support of Ike meant that he would now have important connections at the White House.

"The 1952 campaign gave Republicans a much-needed shot in the arm," Ford says. "The Eisenhower-Nixon ticket helped our candidates everywhere and, for the first time since 1946, we won control of the house."

Minority leader Joseph W. Martin, Jr., of Massachusetts was elected Speaker. He promptly appointed Gerald Ford chairman of the Army panel on the Defense Subcommittee.

During those busy early years, as Jerry steadily climbed

the ladder of success, his young family was growing too. A son, Michael, was born on March 15, 1950, while Jerry and Betty were still living in their first Washington apartment on Q Street in Georgetown.

The apartment had been cozy with just the two of them, but now it was cramped. They moved to a larger place, a garden apartment in a big, park-like complex across the Potomac River in Alexandria, Virginia. A second son, John, came along on March 16, 1952, and even the new apartment seemed crowded with cribs and high chairs, diaper pails and changing tables, toys and tricycles.

For the first few years in Washington, Jerry and Betty kept a home in Grand Rapids and commuted back and forth between the home district and the capital. But, as Mike and Jack grew into active toddlers, the travel grew more and more difficult. Mike would soon be starting school, and Betty wanted to settle down.

There was a new development opening up in Alexandria, not far from their apartment complex. The Fords liked Alexandria and decided to invest in a building lot at 514 Crown View Drive. They found plans for a split-level style they liked and hired contractors to put up a modest brick home on their lot.

Soon after moving into the new house a third son, Steven, was born on May 19, 1956. A fourth child, Susan, came along the next year, on July 6, 1957. Susan was born during the "seventh inning stretch" of a Washington Senators baseball game, Betty remembers. Jerry had promised to take Mike and Steve to the Saturday afternoon game and he didn't want to disappoint them, so he dropped Betty off at the hospital on the way, promising to get back right after the game was over. After the seventh inning he called the hospital to check on Betty's progress and learned that Susan had arrived moments before.

Betty Ford was responsible for most of the day-to-day child rearing, since Jerry was busier and busier every year with his congressional duties. She was lucky to have the help of a woman named Clara Powell, who worked as a housekeeper but quickly became a trusted family friend and second mother to the children.

"As parents, Betty and I tried to give our four children both roots and wings," Ford says. "The roots of family, heritage, and values so they'd know who they were and in what they believed; and wings, the courage to seek personal challenges and the capacity to make it on their own."

By 1954, the Democrats had regained control of the House and something called the Cold War was raging. The Cold War was the nickname given to the chilly war of words and the icy relationships between the United States and its allies, and the Soviet Union and its Communist satellite countries behind the Iron Curtain.

A Senator from Wisconsin, by the name of Joseph McCarthy, was becoming famous as an anti-Communist crusader. He held highly publicized hearings in the Senate, where he charged that the federal government was riddled with Communist subversives and sympathizers. He fed Americans with a daily diet of accusations, hurling charges of Communism at officials in all levels of government.

"People who should have known better tolerated him because they felt that *someone* had to alert the nation to the Communist threat," Ford says. "They acknowledged that his tactics were deplorable, but excused him because they thought he had a worthwhile goal.

"I thought he was a professional bully and I detested him personally, so I kept my distance from him." Looking back, Jerry Ford later decided he had been wrong, that he should have taken McCarthy on and tried to stop him. Even though many others also remained silent about "McCarthyism," as it came to be called, Ford doesn't excuse himself. "The fact that I didn't speak out against McCarthy is a real regret," he says.

That, however, was his only regret. His career was continuing to progress. He was appointed to a special subcommittee that controlled funding for the Central Intelligence Agency (CIA). His own seat in Congress seemed safe, with the voters at home returning him to Congress with wider margins of victory each time, so he was able to campaign in other districts for Republican candidates.

In 1958, in spite of the help Jerry tried to give Republicans, the party took a "terrible licking" at the polls. One of the big reasons, Jerry and some of his fellow Republican congressmen thought, was the "old and tired image that the party was projecting."

A group of younger House members, nicknamed the Young Turks, believed that the party's leaders should come up with constructive alternatives to Democratic programs instead of just working against Democratic bills.

When Democrat John F. Kennedy beat Richard M. Nixon for the presidency in 1960, Jerry Ford and the other Young Turks decided it was time for stronger Republican leadership in the House. They started with the third ranking minority job, the position of Republican Conference Chairman. Early in 1963, Jerry was picked to challenge the chairman and won by a narrow margin.

Two times Jerry had chances to run for higher office, one time for the Senate and once for governor of Michigan. Although both offers were tempting and Jerry briefly considered each of them, he eventually decided to stay right where he was and continue pursuing his goal of becoming Speaker of the House.

Then came an interlude spawned by tragedy. President John F. Kennedy was shot and killed while riding in a motorcade through the streets of Dallas, Texas, on November 22, 1963. The new president, Lyndon Johnson, appointed a distinguished team of seven members, headed by Supreme Court Chief Justice Earl Warren, to investigate the assassination and to make a definitive report to the American people. The president picked Jerry Ford as one of the members of the Warren Commission.

It took six months of intensive investigation for the Warren Commission to reach its conclusion, that the assassination of President Kennedy had been the work of a single murderer, Lee Harvey Oswald. The commission's report was a thick book filled with facts, figures, charts, tables, and reasons.

President Johnson was elected to a term of his own in a landslide victory over Republican Barry Goldwater in 1964. It seemed to the Young Turks that the party leadership needed a serious overhaul. This time the target of their rebellion was the minority leadership, the top Republican job in the house. The minority leader would become Speaker of the House if a Republican house could ever be elected.

When the House was organized in January, 1965, Jerry Ford challenged the incumbent Charles Halleck for the job and won by a slim margin. He had almost reached his goal. Now came the years of challenge.

As minority leader, Jerry Ford worked to find Republican plans that would work better than the "Great Society" programs that President Johnson was trying to push through Congress. As the politicians grappled with the great issues of the times—the war in Vietnam, civil rights, the War on Poverty—the political give-and-take escalated under Ford's leadership.

Jerry fought especially hard against Johnson's big spending programs. "A government big enough to give us everything we wanted," he said, "would also be big enough to take away from us everything we had."

The Republicans tried to replace the War on Poverty with a program they called the Opportunity Crusade. They were successful enough at amending the Johnson programs that they prompted the president to quip, in a moment of frustration, that, "Jerry Ford's a nice guy, but he played football too long without a helmet."

The next time Minority Leader Ford gave a speech at the Gridiron Club, a press club in Washington, he held up the leather helmet he had worn at Michigan. Jerry Ford ended that same 1968 speech with a prophetic joke.

"I'm not at all interested in the vice presidency," he said. "I love the House of Representatives, despite the long, irregular hours. Sometimes, though, when it's late and I'm tired and hungry—on that long drive home to Alexandria—as I go past 1600 Pennsylvania Avenue, I do seem to hear a little voice saying: 'If you lived there, you'd be home by now.' "

The new Republican efforts at leadership paid off with the election of Richard Nixon to the presidency in 1968. Jerry Ford began to hope that the next election would bring the fruition of his dreams, a Republican majority in the House and the Speakership for him. But, when Nixon was returned to office by one of the biggest landslides in history in 1972 and the House still remained solidly Democratic, Jerry realized that his dream couldn't come true. He decided to retire. He would run in 1974 for one last term.

But two major scandals were to rock the nation and change the life of Jerry Ford. The first was a scandal involving Spiro Agnew, the vice president. And the second was Watergate, which involved the president himself.

Agnew was a former governor of Maryland. In the summer and fall of 1973, he was investigated by state officials who suspected that he had taken bribes. As the investigations continued, the evidence seemed to show that Agnew had accepted bribes and kickbacks not only when he was governor, but also as vice president of the United States. Faced with sure criminal prosecution, and desperate to stay out of jail, Agnew made a deal with the prosecutors. He would resign, plead "no contest" to a single reduced charge, and accept probation.

In the meantime, the Nixon White House was under increasing suspicion of having been behind the burglary of Democratic headquarters in the Watergate building. A special committee in the Senate was investigating, and Nixon's presidency was beginning to unravel.

When Agnew resigned, Nixon was required, under the terms of a recent constitutional amendment, to appoint a replacement who would then be approved by Congress. Nixon needed someone who shared his political ideals but who had an absolutely clean record, someone who was completely untainted by scandal. He also needed someone who was well-liked in Congress, someone who could be quickly confirmed without controversy.

That someone turned out to be Jerry Ford. Ford's appointment as vice president was announced by Nixon at a nationally televised White House ceremony on October 12, 1973. Now it was up to Congress, which promptly started confirmation hearings.

In the scandal-weary mood of the times, Ford became one of the most investigated men in United States history. Three hundred and fifty special agents of the FBI interviewed more than a thousand witnesses and issued 1,700 pages of reports. Experts pored over Ford's financial records and combed his past. He was questioned in detail about every aspect of his political life.

"The process was like undergoing a physical exam in public view," Ford says. "Still, the American people wound up knowing more about me than any other nominee is history."

Congress gave Jerry Ford a clean bill of health and, on November 27, 1973, he was confirmed by a huge majority. The swearing-in ceremony took place in the Capitol right after the congressional vote. The new vice president then stood before his former colleagues to speak.

"I am a Ford, not a Lincoln," he said, promising that, if he couldn't speak with the simple elegance of Lincoln, he could at least strive to be Lincoln's equal in honesty and plain speaking.

8

The Thirty-Eighth President, a Time to Heal

Ford's seven-month vice presidency was a tightrope time of walking a fine line between loyalty to President Nixon, whom he still believed to be innocent of any wrongdoing in Watergate, and his responsibility to seek the truth on behalf of the American people.

It was also a time when the spotlight of public attention shone brightly on the Ford family and life in the modest home in Alexandria. Reporters tried to learn everything they could about the Fords. They photographed Mike, a theological student in Boston, and his wife, Gayle. They interviewed Jack, a college student studying forestry in Utah. The third son, Steve, was taking some time off between high school and college and was working as a wrangler on a western ranch. But most of the attention was focused on Susan, a pretty high school student with long, blond hair and a sunny disposition.

The house on Crown View Lane was surrounded by reporters and television news crews. The Secret Service moved in, and the Fords had to convert their garage into a headquarters. The lawn became a tangle of television cables, and traffic on the quiet residential street increased a hundred-fold.

Throughout the spring and early summer of 1974 the Watergate investigations continued, and the American public was bombarded with one shocking revelation after another. Finally, in early August, Nixon decided to resign.

When Gerald R. Ford became the thirty-eighth president he knew that he had a big job ahead of him.

"The oath I have taken is the same oath that was taken by George Washington and by every president under the Constitution. But I assume the presidency under extraordinary circumstances never before experienced by Americans. This is an hour of history that troubles our minds and hurts our hearts," he said to the people of America in his inaugural address.

"I am indebted to no man, and only to one woman, my dear wife, as I begin the most difficult job in the world," he continued, seeking to reassure the country that he had reached the presidency without accumulating any political debts along the way.

"I have not sought this enormous responsibility, but I will not shirk it," he promised. He urged the people to cooperate with his new administration, saying, "We must go forward, now, together."

The new president went on to reassure our foreign allies that he pledged "an uninterrupted and sincere search for peace," adding that America would remain strong and united but that its strength would be dedicated to peace.

Ford promised an open administration, saying "truth is the glue that holds government together" and "honesty is always the best policy in the end."

"My fellow Americans, our long national nightmare is over," the president continued. "Our constitution works; our great republic is a government of laws and not of men. Here the people rule."

He called on the people to help bind the wounds of Watergate, to "restore the golden rule to our political process,

Gerald Ford is sworn in as the thirty-eighth president of the United States by Chief Justice Warren Burger as Mrs. Ford looks on, August 9, 1974. Courtesy of Gerald R. Ford Library

and let brotherhood purge our hearts of suspicion and of hate."

In the closing of his short inaugural speech, he asked for the prayers of Americans for Richard Nixon and his family. "May our former president, who brought peace to millions, find it for himself." He concluded by promising "to do the very best I can for America. God helping me, I will not let you down."

Most Americans found Ford's speech reassuring and supported his efforts to heal the nation. They were tired of scandal and anxious for Ford to lead them to better times.

What were the issues facing the new president? The combination of inflation and high unemployment, a bewildering economic crisis that had been nicknamed "stagflation," was the biggest single problem facing the country. An energy crisis was looming on the horizon, and there were plenty of social programs that needed attention.

Overseas, there were other problems. The Nixon administration had ended the U.S. involvement in the Vietnam War, but tensions in that part of the world remained high, and renewed conflict could shatter the Paris peace accords. The same was true of the Middle East. "The Yom Kippur War of October 1973 had ended in an uneasy truce," Ford said. "Another war could explode at any time."

Ford was also worried about our relationships with the Soviet Union and China. It was time, he felt, to build upon the base of detente that had been created by Nixon.

"These challenges were sufficient to test the mettle of any chief executive, but I think it's fair to say that I took office with a set of unique disadvantages," Ford said. "Normally, Presidents have about seventy-five days of grace between their election and their inauguration. They use this 'shakedown' period to recruit members of their Cabinet and staff and to decide their legislative priorities. I didn't have that luxury, and the lack of a normal transition time caused problems right away. Many of the Nixon holdovers on the White House staff were saying, 'Here comes Jerry Ford and his minor leaguers. Once we settle them down and show them how this game is played, everything will be all right.' And my own people were saying, 'As soon as we get rid of these Nixon appointees, the government will be legitimate again.' "

Ford was aware of what he labeled the seasonal cycle to a presidency. Usually, his theory went, new presidents have their first year in office to lay out their programs for the country. Then, during the second and third years of the term, the president tries to convince Congress to make the laws necessary to get the programs rolling. During the fourth year, the president "mends his fences politically and runs for re-election." Ford had only half that time, and it seemed like he had twice as much to accomplish.

But he had some advantages, too. The people of the country were anxious to forget Watergate and to get on with the business of healing. They were relieved and pleased to have a new, more open president. Rarely had a new president enjoyed such popularity as Ford did during his first month in office.

One of Ford's first moves as president was to go to the Capitol and ask Congress for its cooperation in the days to come. "My fellow Americans, we have a lot of work to do. My former colleagues, you and I have a lot of work to do. Let's get on with it," he said in a speech on the Monday after he took office.

He ended his speech with a resounding tribute to all Americans and a pledge to serve each one to the best of his ability. "I want to be a good president. I need your help. We all need God's sure guidance. With it, nothing can stop the United States of America."

When typical Americans were asked by scientific researchers for their opinions about President Ford, a staggering 97 percent said that they approved of the job he was doing. No other modern president had even approached such a high rate of approval. The Ford presidency was starting out with high hopes and the affectionate goodwill of the American people.

During that first month, Ford plunged into his job with energy and enthusiasm. He announced his choice of a new vice president, Nelson Rockefeller, a former governor of New York and one of the world's wealthiest men. The choice of Rockefeller, a liberal Republican, would be unpopular with many of Ford's conservative supporters, but Ford knew that he needed a strong-minded vice president, so he went ahead with the appointment. He was showing his independence and flexing his presidential muscles.

He traveled to Chicago to talk to a convention of the Veterans of Foreign Wars. There, in the spirit of forgiveness and healing, he announced a limited amnesty program for the draft-dodgers and military deserters of the Vietnam era. He had deliberately picked a group that would likely be opposed to such a move because, he said, "announcing it to them would indicate strength on my part. The Chicago address was the right occasion."

Ford was making a good impression on his fellow Americans. Even those who disagreed with his positions on the issues found him to be refreshingly honest. And they were reassured by his decisiveness and his "take charge" attitude.

But all that was to change. A month after he took office President Ford took a sudden, unexpected, and controversial step. He granted a pardon to former President Nixon for "all offenses against the United States which he, Richard Nixon, has committed or may have committed or taken part in during the period from January 20, 1969, through August 9, 1974."

The pardon privilege is a right given presidents by the Constitution to officially forgive crimes that have been committed. It is intended as one more of the "checks and balances" that are the foundation of our government. In this case the president can overrule the judicial system. He is a last avenue of appeal, a sort of safety valve. The power of a president to grant pardons would insure, the writers of the constitution hoped, that there would be room for mercy and forgiveness in our system of government.

Ford had decided to pardon Nixon because "my conscience tells me clearly and certainly that I cannot prolong the bad dreams that continue to reopen a chapter that is closed. My conscience tells me that only I, as president, have the constitutional power to firmly shut and seal this book. My conscience tells me that it is my duty not merely to proclaim domestic tranquility but to use every means to insure it," he said when he announced the pardon.

"I was very sure of what would happen if I let the charges against Nixon run their legal course," Ford later explained. "Months were sure to elapse between indictment and trial. The entire process would no doubt require years: a minimum of two, a maximum of six. And Nixon would not spend time quietly in San Clemente. He would be fighting for his freedom, taking his cause to the people, and his constant struggle

President Ford wears a "WIN" button during a Rose Garden press conference on October 9, 1974.
Courtesy of Gerald R. Ford Library

would have dominated the news.

"The story would overshadow everything else. No other issue could compete with the drama of a former president trying to stay out of jail. It would be virtually impossible for me to direct public attention to anything else. Passions on both sides would be aroused. A period of such prolonged vituperation and recrimination would be disastrous for the nation. America needed recovery, not revenge."

Once Ford had decided that the pardon was necessary, he saw no reason to wait. "To procrastinate, to agonize, and to wait for a more favorable turn of events," he said, "is a weak and potentially dangerous course for a president to follow."

Sunday morning, September 8, 1974, was the time he planned to make his announcement. "Once I determine to move, I seldom, if ever, fret. I have confidence that my lifetime batting average is high, and I'm prepared to live with the consequences," he said.

He went to church to pray for wisdom; then, determined and calm, he returned to his office. There he reviewed the text of his speech and made a few changes. He called leaders of Congress and other officials whom he thought should be informed of the pardon ahead of time. Finally, just before eleven o'clock on that Sunday morning, he faced the television cameras and announced his decision to the American people.

Ford had not expected the pardon to be popular, and he knew that he would be criticized for it, but he was convinced that he had done the right thing.

Reaction was swift and stunning. The pardon was roundly denounced by congressmen and senators, news columnists and commentators, government workers and private citizens, Republicans and Democrats, friends and foes. Even Ford's press secretary, Jerald F. terHorst, a good friend for most of his political life, resigned in protest.

The negative reaction swelled as the news spread. Some critics even charged that there had been a "deal" between Nixon and Ford, that Nixon had traded the presidency for a pardon.

For the first time, Ford was picketed by angry protestors. "Jail Ford, jail Ford," some angry demonstrators chanted. The White House received almost four thousand letters in less than a week, most of them against the pardon. And Ford's popularity in the public opinion polls plunged to 49 percent.

The president was astonished and dismayed. "I began to wonder whether, instead of healing the wounds, my decision had only rubbed salt in them."

Ford wanted to reassure the nation that there had been no deal between him and Nixon, so he did something no president had done before. He appeared before a congressional sub-committee and testified under oath about his reasons for the pardon. That action helped somewhat to tone down the great outcry, but the pardon was to remain controversial and troublesome to Ford throughout his presidency.

Then came another crisis, this time in the family. When Betty, who was proving to be a popular and candid first lady, went for a routine medical checkup, a lump was discovered on her breast. Ford was given the news by the White House doctor, who told him that Mrs. Ford would have to have surgery as soon as possible.

The lump would be removed. Some of the tissue from the lump would be examined under a microscope to see if any cancer cells were present. If the lump turned out to be cancerous, or malignant, the doctors would remove the breast in an operation called a mastectomy.

After talking with the doctor, Ford went to his wife, put his arms around her, and kissed her tenderly. He told her he was sure that everything would be all right, even though he was secretly terrified.

"We were lucky she'd had the examination," he said. "And now we were luckier still that she was going to receive the very best care."

Mrs. Ford's surgery was scheduled for Saturday, September 28, 1974. On Friday evening, after she had completed her full schedule for the day, Betty Ford checked into Bethesda Naval Medical Center in nearby Maryland.

"That night was the loneliest in my life," Ford remembers. "The thought that the woman I loved might be taken away from me was almost too much to endure."

The next morning, a dismal, rainy day, Ford was given the news that the lump was cancerous and that a radical mastectomy had been performed. He had been working on a speech with one of his assistants, Robert Hartmann, when the doctor called. Ford excused himself and went into the small office bathroom where he struggled to control his feelings. When he returned to his desk, Hartmann could tell just how torn up the president was by the expression on his face.

"Go ahead and cry," the assistant said.

"All my tensions and fears poured out in a brief flood of tears," Ford recalls. But after crying, he felt a little better. He went immediately to the hospital to be with his wife as she came out of the anesthetic.

"Gradually, over the next week or ten days, Betty's condition improved," President Ford said. "Her adjustment to the diagnosis and to the mastectomy was superb. She had one brief bout of postoperative depression, but she never lapsed into self-pity. Instead, she decided to be completely candid about what had happened to her. She was warmed by the news that cancer clinics around the country were reporting a significant increase in the number of women who came in for physical examinations. She knew the publicity about her mastectomy was a factor and that it could help save lives. I was enormously proud of her."

9

On the Campaign Trail Again

Soon after assuming the presidency, Gerald Ford decided that he would run for a term of his own in the 1976 election. There were several reasons for his decision. First of all, he loved being president and had decided he was good at it.

And Secretary of State Kissinger had convinced him that he must run again. If he didn't, Kissinger urged, it would be a disaster from a foreign policy point of view. For the next two and a half years all the foreign governments would know they were dealing with a lame-duck president, one who would not be back. The foreign leaders would defer important decisions.

"All our initiatives would be dead in the water, and I wouldn't be able to implement your foreign policy," Kissinger lamented. He also outlined potential domestic consequences, saying that any announcement of retirement plans by Ford or any indication that he wouldn't be running again would touch off a scramble for the nomination among the Republicans who were needed to support Ford's policies.

"Henry was right," Ford says. "The moment I said I wasn't going to run, the succession struggle would start. That would be divisive in and of itself, and what the country needed was a period of stability."

Now, committed to seek another term, Jerry Ford settled into office. The job of a president is a daily grind of duties that range from ceremonial tasks such as welcoming a visiting beauty queen to the management of serious crises. The president must meet with his staff each day, delegate chores to subordinates, communicate with Congress, meet with the leaders of other nations, and try to solve the myriad problems that face the nation at any given time.

Throughout his administration, Ford's relationship with Congress grew worse as he sought the cooperation of his former colleagues in pushing through programs he thought important. Unfortunately, the Democrats in Congress, as much as they might admire Jerry Ford personally, were not inclined to help him by passing Republican programs.

President Ford, in his short two and a half year term, so overshadowed by the ghosts of Watergate, did not have time to build effective programs of his own to take to Congress. He tried to halt the relentless erosion of the dollar caused by inflation with a program called WIN, which stood for Whip Inflation Now.

The WIN program, which called for private citizens to help in the battle by cutting back on spending and increasing their savings, was a failure. Critics said that WIN was a shallow public relations gesture that did nothing to get at the roots of inflation.

Congress did not respond to the president's requests to cut spending either, so the president vetoed many spending programs that he felt to be irresponsible. A law passed by Congress does not go into effect until the president signs it. When the president refuses to sign a bill, it is called a veto. But Congress can override a presidential veto by getting two-thirds of its members to vote for the vetoed bill. Then it becomes law anyway.

And that's what Congress did, over and over again. Jerry Ford, the former congressman, got a bitter taste of his own medicine as he continued to battle with his old friends on Capitol Hill.

Faced with the frustration of an obstructionist Congress

President Ford and Soviet General Secretary Leonid I. Brezhnev in Vladivostok, USSR, November 23, 1974.
Courtesy of Gerald R. Ford Library

at home, Ford turned to foreign relations as an area to assert his lagging leadership. In November of 1974, he traveled to Japan, becoming the first American president ever to do so.

Ford also visited the Soviet Union, where he met with Communist chief Leonid Brezhnev and forged a basic agreement for a new peace treaty that would limit the production and deployment of nuclear weapons.

Ford had the misfortune to preside over one of the saddest chapters in American history, the fall of Vietnam. He was forced to watch helplessly from the White House as the Communists from North Vietnam invaded the south. American

President Ford listens to advisors at a July 19, 1975, National Security Council meeting called during the Mayaguez *incident. Official White House photo by David Hume Kennerly*

prestige fell to a new low as Saigon fell to the Communist forces and the last Americans were evacuated from the roof of the U.S. embassy by helicopter.

Ford asked Congress to authorize him to send military help to the South Vietnamese, but Congress, anxious to end once and for all the long war that had so divided the nation, refused. The governments of Cambodia and Laos quickly collapsed after the fall of South Vietnam, and the bitter years of the Vietnam War ended on a note of despair. The long war had divided the nation against itself, had cost billions of dollars, and more than 56,000 American lives.

Ford's popularity at home plummeted along with American prestige abroad. Then Cambodian Communists captured an American merchant ship, the freighter *Mayaguez,* on May 12, 1975. President Ford, determined to prove that there were limits to America's willingness to be pushed around,

President Ford signing the Final Act of the Conference on Security and Cooperation in Europe, in Helsinki, Finland, August 1, 1975. Courtesy of Gerald R. Ford Library

ordered the Navy to rescue the captured ship and her thirty-nine crewmen.

On May 15, U.S. Marines were helicoptered to the island where the crew was believed to be held. An invasion force of Marines boarded the captured ship and searched for the crew. Later that day the Cambodians released the freighter's crew unharmed, but the incident had cost forty-one American lives. Nevertheless, it had been necessary to prove, Ford asserted, that Americans would not stand for such unbridled Communist aggression.

The *Mayaguez* helped to restore some of Ford's popularity at home and some of the nation's failed prestige abroad. But Ford believed the Communists needed further convincing that the United States meant to continue its resistance to Communist aggression. He embarked on a series of trips abroad to meet with world leaders and to reinforce the American position.

President and Mrs. Ford with Chinese Vice Chairman Deng Xiao Ping in Peking, December 3, 1975.
Courtesy of Gerald R. Ford Library

In Helsinki, Finland, Ford met with the leaders of thirty-three other nations to sign a treaty, often called the Helsinki Accords, that guaranteed that the borders of European nations would remain the same as they had at the end of World War II. The accords also spelled out agreements on basic human rights for the citizens of all the signatory nations, including most of the Iron Curtain countries.

Late in 1975, Ford traveled to China, where he attempted to build upon the goodwill between Americans and the Chinese that Nixon had begun. Ford was welcomed warmly by Chinese leaders, but wasn't able to reach any important new agreements.

At home, public opinion polls showed that the president was unlikely to be reelected in 1976. He might not even win the Republican nomination, the polls predicted. Another Republican, Ronald Reagan, former governor of California, planned to challenge Ford in the primary elections.

President Ford meets with Egyptian President Anwar Sadat in Salzburg, Austria, June 2, 1975. Courtesy of Gerald R. Ford Library

Ford began an active campaign to save his job. He hired public relations specialists to help him improve his image. He contacted supporters and asked for help. He traveled all over the country to give speeches, to speak out on the issues, and to enlist the support of the public.

He took his campaign to California and into the backyard of his major competitor, Ronald Reagan. It was in California that he faced death at the hands of assassins on two separate occasions less than two weeks apart.

The first attempt came on September 5, as the president made his way through a crowd in Sacramento. A young woman by the name of Lynette ("Squeaky") Fromme, a devoted follower of convicted mass murderer Charles Manson, raised a loaded Colt .45 and took dead aim at the president. Ford spotted the gun and ducked, using his quick athletic reflexes. At the same time Secret Service agents wrestled the woman to the ground and disarmed her.

"Squeaky Fromme," Ford later wrote, "was an aberration. There had been misfits and kooks in every society since the beginning of time. I didn't think California harbored a larger number of these people than any other part of the country, so I wasn't overly concerned about my personal safety when I returned to the state on September 19."

He campaigned hard in California for three days—participating in ceremonies at two universities, speaking at an insurance convention, meeting political leaders, and shaking a lot of hands. On September 22, he spoke to members of a major union and attended a luncheon of the Northern California World Affairs Council in a San Francisco hotel.

Outside the hotel, after the luncheon, Ford walked toward the limousine that was waiting to take him to the airport. He wanted to shake a few hands in the crowd that watched from across the street, but Secret Service agents advised against it, so he waved instead and continued toward the car.

"Bang! I recognized the sound of a shot and I froze. There was a hushed silence for a split second, then pandemonium broke out," Ford remembers.

By tradition, each president of the United States since William Howard Taft has served as honorary president of the Boy Scouts of America. President Ford, the first president to have been an Eagle Scout, is right at home in his uniform.
Courtesy of Boy Scouts of America

President Ford rings the ship's bell of the USS Forrestal *on July 4, 1976 to celebrate the 200th birthday of the United States of America.*
Courtesy of Gerald R. Ford Library

An alert bystander deflected the shot and the assailant, a woman named Sara Jane Moore, was captured by the swarming Secret Service agents. Ford was pushed into the armored limousine and rushed to the airport and into the security of the presidential plane, Air Force One.

Betty Ford, who had been visiting friends, boarded Air Force One shortly after her husband. She had not been listening to the news and knew nothing about the second assassination attempt. When she entered the cabin she looked at her Jerry and smiled. "Well, how did they treat you in San Francisco?" she asked.

A welcome relief from the pressures of campaigning was the celebration of America's two hundredth birthday, its bicentennial. President Ford participated in celebrations all across the country, often combining the ceremonial duties with campaign messages.

It seemed ironic and inspiring that America's bicentennial

President Ford campaigning in Cleveland, Ohio, in October, 1976.
A presidential campaign is a long, grueling series of visits to cities
and towns, factories and farms, conventions and meetings, parties
and parades all across the country.
Courtesy of Gerald R. Ford Library

president should be an unelected one who had reached the
presidency via the disgrace of his predecessor. At the same
time, Gerald Ford was inspiring presidential proof of the
stability of our democracy and the wisdom of our Constitution.

During the first half of 1976, Ford and Reagan were locked
in a tight race for the Republican nomination. They battled
through the long primary season and down to the wire at the
Republican convention. Ford, in an effort to shore up his
lagging support among conservatives, changed his stance on
a number of issues.

At the convention in Kansas City, he narrowly won the
nomination on a first ballot victory with only 1,187 votes to
Reagan's 1,070. The Democrats nominated a newcomer to
the national political scene, a former governor of Georgia
named Jimmy Carter. The battle lines were drawn, and the
race was on.

Dressed in costumes of their ancestral country, Poland, pupils of a Polish Saturday School pose with President Ford during a campaign visit to Buffalo, New York.

Buffalo Courier-Express *photo by Bob Bukaty, courtesy of E.H. Butler Library, State University College at Buffalo and the Historical Society of Buffalo and Erie County*

President Ford stops to congratulate the bride and groom at a wedding reception in Buffalo, New York, while on a campaign swing through the state just before the 1976 election.
Buffalo Courier-Express *photo by Bob Bukaty, courtesy of E.H. Butler Library, State University College at Buffalo and the Historical Society of Buffalo and Erie County*

Polls showed that Carter was way ahead of Ford. Once again advisors were telling Jerry Ford that he didn't have a chance. But Ford continued to fight, and the gap between him and Carter began to slowly close.

Ford challenged Carter to a series of debates, the first such debates between an incumbent and challenger. The first debate helped Ford, who appeared calm, assured, and thoroughly presidential throughout. Carter, by contrast, seemed nervous and defensive. Ford's standing in the polls crept upward.

In the second debate, however, Ford made a disastrous mistake when he erroneously claimed the Soviet Union did

Campaigning means shaking hands, as any politician knows. Gerald Ford is an "old hand" at the job.
Buffalo Courier-Express *photo courtesy of E.H. Butler Library, State University College at Buffalo and the Historical Society of Buffalo and Erie County*

not dominate the nations of Eastern Europe. His popularity slipped again.

But Carter was having problems, too, and the race remained close. Ford did well in the third and final debate. He continued to campaign with renewed energy, crisscrossing the country, putting everything he had into this last whirlwind attempt to convince the American public to give him a second chance.

The gap between the two candidates narrowed. By election day the race was too close to call. Pollster George Gallup called Ford's campaign "the greatest comeback in the history of public-opinion polling."

Three Scouts, representing the Boy Scouts of America, present the national organization's annual report to President Ford, who served, like other U.S. presidents, as honorary Scout president.
Courtesy of Boy Scouts of America

The Ford family in the Oval Office following the president's conces-
sion to Jimmy Carter, November 3, 1976. Family members left to
right, are Steve, Jack, Betty Ford, President Ford, Susan, Gayle
(Mrs. Michael Ford) and Mike.
Courtesy of Gerald R. Ford Library

On election day the voters turned out in moderate numbers
to cast their ballots. When the polls closed and the nation's
will was done, Gerald Ford had lost an extremely close race.

The next morning, when the last votes had been counted
and the results were known, Ford telephoned Carter to offer
his congratulations. Then the first family gathered in the Oval
Office to concede the election in front of the television cameras. Ford had lost his voice from so much campaigning, so
Betty read the poignant concession statement.

The rest of Gerald R. Ford's presidency was devoted to
effecting a smooth transition between his administration and
the incoming administration of Jimmy Carter. In his last

speech to Congress, Ford expressed pride in his achievements and hope for the future.

"I am proud of the part I have had in rebuilding confidence in the presidency, confidence in our free system, and confidence in our future," he said in his final State of the Union address on January 12, 1977. "Once again Americans believe in themselves, in their leaders, and in the promise that tomorrow holds for their children."

10

After the Presidency

It was Inauguration Day again. This time, it was a typical inauguration program in frosty January. There would be festive parades, grand balls, and all the other celebrations that normally accompany the swearing in of a new president of the United States.

Gerald R. Ford stood on the special platform that had been built in front of the Capitol. From there he could see where the Washington Monument stands, straight and timeless, reaching toward the clear Washington sky. Thousands of Americans jammed the grounds below, waiting for the time-honored ceremony to begin.

President Ford swallowed hard and tried to will the tense lines of his face into relaxation. His expression was somber as he watched the man who had defeated him place his hand on the Bible and prepare to recite the same oath Ford had taken on that muggy August afternoon only two and a half years before.

"I, Jimmy Carter, do solemnly swear . . . "

After the oath had been administered, Ford sat quietly to listen to Carter's inaugural address. The first words were an unexpected tribute: "For myself and for our nation, I want to thank my predecessor for all he has done to heal our land."

"That was so unexpected, such a gracious thing for him to say," Ford says. "The crowd began to applaud, and I bit my lip to mask my emotions. I didn't know whether to remain seated or to stand. But when the cheers continued I decided to stand, and I reached over to clasp Carter's hand."

After the inaugural ceremony, the former president and his wife left the Capitol and boarded the helicopter that would take them to Andrews Air Force Base, where a plane awaited to take them to retirement in California.

The helicopter flight usually took no longer than ten minutes, but Ford asked the pilot to circle slowly over the Capitol dome one final time. "That's my real home," the former president said quietly as he gazed on the inspiring view.

At Andrews Air Force Base a crowd was waiting to wish the Fords farewell. A small band played "God Bless America," and enthusiastic well-wishers waved signs that read "Good Luck" and "Thank You, Jerry." All the members of his cabinet were there. So were the Rockefellers and the Kissingers. Ford gave each of these special friends a brief hug and shook hands with everyone.

Then he and Betty boarded the plane, a backup to Air Force One. "The mood aboard that plane was high-spirited and extremely festive at first," Ford remembers. "Everyone was trying to crack jokes and laugh. We still were exhilarated by the warmth of the crowd's response."

The airliner streaked west across the sky above America, following the sun. "Halfway across the country," Ford says, "it was as if an invisible force had entered the plane. The merriment ceased, and people began returning to their seats. Betty and I were sitting up forward in our private compartment, and I reached out to hold her hand."

Ford's thoughts traveled back in time, to a dreary morning in August, 1974, when he was first told that President Nixon was thinking of resigning. "I remembered how cloudy it had been in Washington that day. Now I looked out the window of the plane. The sun was shining brightly. I couldn't see a cloud anywhere, and I felt glad about that."

The plane brought the Fords to Palm Springs, California,

As a former president, Gerald Ford is in frequent demand as a public speaker. He often supports Republican candidates for office and makes public appearances on their behalf, usually making an important contribution to their victory. The immensely popular Ford is usually greeted by cheering crowds.

Buffalo Courier-Express photo courtesy E. H. Butler Library, State University College at Buffalo and the Historical Society of Buffalo and Erie County and to a new life, one that would bring its own challenges. Jerry Ford was scheduled to play in a golf tournament at Pebble Beach the next day. Then the Fords planned to fly to Houston, Texas, to attend a memorial dinner for football coach Vince Lombardi. They had agreed to go because the purpose of the dinner was to raise funds for cancer research. Now Ford wondered if the organizers of the dinner would be happy with an ex-president.

He asked Betty what she thought. "Don't worry, darling," Mrs. Ford replied with a laugh. "It's me they're coming to see."

Even though she had been joking, Betty was probably right. Since her early days in the White House, when she had been outspoken and forthright about the issues that concerned her and since her courageous fight against cancer, Betty Ford was one of the most popular women in America.

The Fords had picked the desert community of Palm Springs to build their new retirement home. One of the reasons for the choice was Betty's arthritis, which had caused her so much trouble and pain over the years. Doctors had suggested that she would be best off in a hot, dry climate.

Susan Ford was living nearby in her own condominium. Sons Jack and Steve were both Californians now. Jack worked in the field of magazine publishing, and Steve held jobs in ranching while he tried to break into the field of acting. He would later land several good roles and become a regular soap opera star as the amiable bartender, Andy Richards, on NBC's *The Young and the Restless*. The Ford's oldest son, Mike, and his wife, Gayle, were living in Pittsburgh, Pennsylvania, since Mike's graduation from theological school.

Gerald Ford was widely respected for his accomplishments as a healer in the Republican party. He was a popular speaker, often earning good fees for his work. He was invited to join the board of directors of several corporations and frequently gave advice to businesses as a consultant. His travel increased after his presidency as he became a senior statesman to the Republican party.

Both Mr. and Mrs. Ford signed million-dollar contracts to

write their autobiographies. Life after the presidency settled
into a pattern of travel, writing, public speaking, golf games,
and business meetings for the former president. Mrs. Ford
spent much of her time on the writing of her autobiography
and on supervising the building of their new home in Rancho
Mirage, near Palm Springs. She found post-presidential life
more stressful than her husband did.

For Betty, life in Rancho Mirage was hauntingly similar
to the lonely days in Alexandria, Virginia, when her husband
was House minority leader and away from home more than
two hundred nights a year.

As the new house took shape and Betty was faced with
the huge job of unpacking the accumulation of a lifetime, the
stress began to build. Her osteoarthritis flared up, causing a
pinched nerve in her neck to inflict periods of excruciating
pain. Betty swallowed countless pills and capsules, which had
been prescribed by her doctors, to fight the pain and tension.
She also continued her usual social drinking of alcoholic bev-
erages. The drugs and the alcohol had a powerful combined
effect, an effect which really worried Susan Ford, who was
helping with the unpacking.

Susan was concerned about her mother's continuing use
of prescription drugs and alcohol. She was so worried that
she confided in a doctor, who suggested an intervention—a
process where the people who love an alcoholic or drug-
dependent person confront their loved one with their concern.

The first intervention took place when Susan; the doctor;
Mrs. Ford's secretary; and Clara Powell, the long-time family
housekeeper and friend, all marched into Betty's sitting room
and tried to talk to her about giving up all medicine and
liquor.

"It was brave of them," Betty Ford wrote in her autobiography, *The Times of My Life,* "but I wasn't in a mood to
admire them for their courage." In fact, Mrs. Ford said, she
was "completely turned off." Experts say that her initial reaction is typical.

Susan called her father, who cancelled his speaking en-

Gerald R. Ford still does a lot of campaigning, this time for other Republican candidates. Here he urges voters to support Ronald Reagan for president. Ford's support helped Reagan win in 1980 and again in 1984.
Buffalo Courier-Express *photo, courtesy of E.H. Butler Library, State University College at Buffalo and the Historical Society of Buffalo and Erie County*

gagements and flew home. She alerted her brothers. The Fords sought the help of Captain Joe Pursch, the Navy doctor who was in charge of an unusually successful drug and alcohol rehabilitation program at the Long Beach Naval Hospital. They decided to try a second intervention.

This time they were successful in convincing Betty Ford to seek professional help for her problems. She agreed to check into the rehabilitation center at Long Beach for a six-week program of therapy. President Ford and other family members also attended programs at Long Beach, where they learned about the twin diseases of alcoholism and drug dependency.

What they learned surprised them. Alcoholism is a disease that affects more than one out of every ten Americans. There is no such thing as a typical alcoholic. The disease can, and does, strike anyone. They learned that it is a disease of denial, that both the victims and their loved ones are typically unwilling to face the facts. They learned that millions of Americans, a large percentage of them women, are dependent on supposedly harmless prescription drugs. Most important, they learned that, while the disease is not curable, it can be stopped. Chemical abusers can learn to give up their addictions and live healthy, drug- and alcohol-free lives.

With typical candor and courage, both President and Mrs. Ford released full information about her disease to the press. After all, thousands of American women had gone to clinics for breast examinations after Betty's mastectomy. Maybe her latest fight would also inspire Americans who suffered from alcoholism or drug addiction to seek help.

Betty's continued recovery from alcoholism and drug dependency has resulted in the construction of a special treatment facility at the Eisenhower Medical Center in Palm Springs. Named after her, the center has served hundreds of recovering addicts. Betty Ford, president of the center's board of directors, devotes almost full-time hours to raising funds for the program and raising the consciousness of the American public.

While Betty Ford continued her recovery, her husband

continued to maintain an active interest in politics. He was, in fact, a prime reason behind the defeat of President Carter after a single term.

Jimmy Carter served for four years as president and then ran for a second term against Gerald Ford's old rival, Ronald Reagan, who finally captured the Republican nomination. Putting old enmity aside, Ford campaigned hard on behalf of Reagan, who went on to win the presidency in 1980 and again in 1984. Many Republicans believe that Gerald R. Ford had healed the Republican party and paved the way for its rebuilding in the 1980s.

Shortly after Ronald Reagan became president of the United States, there was a tragedy in Egypt. Anwar Sadat, Egypt's president, was assassinated, struck down by a hail of bullets as he reviewed a military parade in Cairo.

It was important that America be represented at the funeral of this friend and ally, who was an important link for the elusive peace in the Middle East. But, the White House decided, it was simply too dangerous for President Reagan to travel to Cairo for the funeral. The region was far too unstable, the situation too volatile, the area too vulnerable to terrorists.

So Reagan made a historic proposal and asked the three living former presidents—Richard Nixon, Gerald Ford, and Jimmy Carter—to make the trip on America's behalf. The three men agreed.

The tension aboard the plane was thick. The three presidents weren't sure what to say to each other. But, as the flight continued and the ice was broken, they found there was plenty to say.

Jerry Ford and Jimmy Carter, after their sad mission was completed, found time to talk about their mutual frustrations in the Middle East. They discussed possibilities for peace. The result of their informal discussion was a joint magazine article they wrote for *Reader's Digest*. Since then, the two former presidents often work together for the cause of peace, sponsoring seminars and debates on the subject and speaking

The boy who overcame a stutter is now one of the country's most popular public speakers. Since he retired from the presidency, Gerald R. Ford has given an average of two hundred speeches a year.

Buffalo Courier-Express *photo, courtesy of E.H. Butler Library, State University College at Buffalo and the Historical Society of Buffalo and Erie County*

out with a unified voice.

In September of 1981, the Gerald Ford Museum was opened in Grand Rapids, Michigan. Ronald Reagan attended the dedication in order to pay tribute to his old rival: "Gerald Ford healed America because he understood the adventure of America: her way of governing, her people, and the source of her strength as a nation."

The Gerald Ford Museum in Grand Rapids and the Gerald R. Ford Library on the campus of the University of Michigan in Ann Arbor, both built with private funds and publicly administered by the national archives, house exhibits and the presidential papers of the Ford administration.

In December, 1985, Gerald R. Ford was honored with the unveiling of a marble bust of himself, which was placed on a pedestal in the halls of the Senate. The sculpture (a massive block of pristine white marble carved by artist Walker Hancock of Massachusetts) was dedicated not to Ford's presidency, but rather to his role as president of the Senate while he was vice president.

Somehow, it seemed especially appropriate to Ford that this tribute to his service to his country was placed in the nation's Capitol, which he considered his "real home." At the dedication ceremonies Ford joked that the statue was better looking than he was in real life. Then, his expression almost as serious as that of the imposing bust behind him, Ford summed up the twenty-five years of his distinguished congressional career: "I had a lot of adversaries, but I don't believe I ever had an enemy."

Index